Suddenly Jewish

Suddenly

Jewish

JEWS RAISED AS GENTILES DISCOVER THEIR JEWISH ROOTS

Barbara Kessel

BRANDEIS UNIVERSITY PRESS

PUBLISHED BY UNIVERSITY PRESS OF NEW ENGLAND

HANOVER & LONDON

BRANDEIS UNIVERSITY PRESS

Published by University Press of New England,

Hanover, NH 03755

Printed in United States of America

CIP data appear at the end of the book

5 4 3 2

Jacket illustration: Norman Rockwell, *Let Nothing You Dismay* (*Ladies Home Journal*, July 1941). Printed by permission of the Norman Rockwell Family Trust

BRANDEIS SERIES IN AMERICAN JEWISH HISTORY, CULTURE, AND LIFE

Jonathan D. Sarna, Editor
Sylvia Barack Fishman, Associate Editor

Leon A. Jick, 1992
The Americanization of the Synagogue, 1820–1870

Sylvia Barack Fishman, editor, 1992
Follow My Footprints: Changing Images of Women in American Jewish Fiction

Gerald Tulchinsky, 1993
Taking Root: The Origins of the Canadian Jewish Community

Shalom Goldman, editor, 1993
Hebrew and the Bible in America: The First Two Centuries

Marshall Sklare, 1993
Observing America's Jews

Reena Sigman Friedman, 1994
These Are Our Children: Jewish Orphanages in the United States, 1880–1925

Alan Silverstein, 1994
Alternatives to Assimilation: The Response of Reform Judaism to American Culture, 1840–1930

Jack Wertheimer, editor, 1995
The American Synagogue: A Sanctuary Transformed

Sylvia Barack Fishman, 1995
A Breathe of Life: Feminism in the American Jewish Community

Diane Matza, editor, 1996

Sephardic-American Voices: Two Hundred Years of a Literary Legacy

Joyce Antler, editor, 1997

Talking Back: Images of Jewish Women in American Popular Culture

Jack Wertheimer, 1997

A People Divided: Judaism in Contemporary America

Beth S. Wenger and Jeffrey Shandler, editors, 1998

Encounters with the "Holy Land": Place, Past and Future in American Jewish Culture

David Kaufman, 1998

Shul with a Pool: The "Synagogue-Center" in American Jewish History

Roberta Rosenberg Farber and Chaim I. Waxman, 1999

Jews in America: A Contemporary Reader

Murray Friedman and Albert D. Chernin, 1999

A Second Exodus: The American Movement to Free Soviet Jews

Stephen J. Whitfield, 1999

In Search of American Jewish Culture

Naomi W. Cohen, 1999

Jacob H. Schiff: A Study in American Jewish Leadership

Barbara Kessel, 2000

Suddenly Jewish: Jews Raised as Gentiles Discover Their Jewish Roots

To my parents,

Marion and Hy Baras, and

Sima and Morris Kessel

For teaching me where I came from;

To Allen

For sharing the voyage;

To Aliza and Jonathan

For continuing the journey;

With thanks to the Almighty,

Without Whom, nothing

CONTENTS

ACKNOWLEDGMENTS

Warm appreciation for so generously sharing their insights, encouragement, and expertise: Joy Bashevkin, Roselyn Bell, Fran Benson, Dr. Evan Imber-Black, Naomi Chiel Bolzman, Rabbi Herbert Bomzer, Susan Borger, Irving Cantor, Deborah Chiel, Phyllis Deutsch, Stephen J. Dubner, Susan Frank, Dr. Elliot Frank, Zena Freundlich, Dr. Usher Freundlich, Judy Goldstein, Judy Hasson, Dr. William Helmreich for his enormously constructive criticism, Joshua Henkin, Dr. Barry Herman, Barbara Hollander, writer James Allan Kennedy, Sandy Kilstein, Maya Kravtsov, Rabbi Stephen J. Lerner, Minna Lipkin, Ann Novick, Harvey Paretzky, Rebecca Rivkin, agent Pesha Rubinstein, Dr. Jonathan Sarna (who has my eternal gratitude), Harriet Schimel, Dr. Lawrence Schiffman, Dr. Jon Stratton, attorney Joseph Tuchinsky, Clara and Dr. Jonas Waizer, Dr. Don Well, and all the people who shared their stories with me.

This book is as much Allen's as it is mine. He relieved me of all earthly burdens so that I could stare at a computer screen for hours and hours, and never touch a bottle of fabric softener.

B.K.

Suddenly Jewish

AUTHOR'S QUERY

For a book on identity, I would like to interview individuals raised as non-Jews who discovered they are of Jewish descent.
Barbara Kessel

Ms. Kessel: Have you interviewed Rabbi Roderick Young? He found out when he was an undergraduate at Oxford that his mother, who raised him Episcopalian/Anglican, is Jewish.

It's probably too late, but I was born in Poland, raised Catholic, immigrated to the US in '59 at age seven, and learned at 22 (the night before my Roman Catholic wedding) that both my parents were Holocaust survivors and that all of our family is Jewish.

Dear Ms. Kessel: I was raised to believe I was the daughter of an Irish-American mother and a Syrian-Palestinian. I learned only three months ago that my biological father is a Jew.

When we found out my family was Jewish, my wife's reaction was, boy, I'm glad you're not an anti-Semite. My first reaction was, I'm glad you're not*!*

Barbara, I have the name and address of a man who was interviewed on Israeli television. As a child, he was hidden in a monastery in France during the Holocaust and found out he was Jewish when he was a young adult studying for the priesthood. He now lives on a religious kibbutz.

Dear Ms. Kessel: You might want to interview my friend. She was adopted by a Jewish couple thirty-eight years ago, when she was six weeks old. Nine years ago she was contacted by her Palestinian birth father. She wrote an article about the tensions that ensued.

How did I feel about it? I was glad to find out I'm Jewish. I got rid of Christmas, Heaven, and Hell—all in the same day!

Prologue

I was born Marcel Pierre Jacques Nakache on March 22, 1939, in Paris to Rita Nakache. She didn't have a husband, and I don't know anything about my father. The original family name was Nekhushtan, from generations back when they lived in Samarkand in the former Soviet Union. The name means copper, so they were probably jewelry makers. They moved to Syria in the 1700s, where they stayed until the Damascus riots in 1840, when the Alliance Française Israelite moved them to France. They were wealthy and very assimilated, so assimilated that my mother converted to Catholicism before I was born and never thought of herself as Jewish.

My mother had me baptized and educated in Catholic boarding schools, which offered the best possible education, so in effect, I never lived with her. She visited once a month, but I never knew a real family life with two parents and siblings. This is not to say I wasn't happy. I was always placed in fine institutions.

I can tell you that in 1944, when I was five years old, I awoke to the sounds of heavy traffic outside the school—trucks and buses. It was most unusual. All of a sudden, one of the Paulist sisters scooped me up and threw me into a laundry bin. She covered me with dirty clothes and told me to be quiet. I don't know how long I was in there. I know I cried and slept, cried and slept. At some point, she pulled me out and hugged me in her arms. I was crying hard and there was nobody around, just the two of us.

"Where did they go?"

"They went on a little outing. They'll be back soon."

"Why does everybody get to go on an outing except me?" I was hurt, confused and envious. They never came back, but other children and staff came and replaced them over the next weeks.

(I went back to that school in 1971, but it was gone. I found some older local people and asked them if they knew what happened that day. One of them told me that the Gestapo found out the school was sheltering Jews, Gypsies and Communists, and to teach them a lesson, they deported the lot. That nun must have hidden the both of us during the raid.)

I was a very good student and an altar boy to age seventeen. I was educated by the Dombosco Order. It's a very ascetic order. They would give me candies, for example, and I would have to give them out to my friends before I ate any. If there was enough left over for me, fine. If not, I had to be happy that I had the opportunity to make others happy, and not complain that there was no candy for me. It was an exercise in learning selflessness. The monks were very tough.

At seventeen, you have to decide what direction your life will take—trade school, professional school, or priesthood. I wanted to be a missionary. I would go anywhere they sent me, but I would have preferred Indochina. I took my exams in Latin, prayer, theology, and did very well. So I chose divinity school. Before you start, you are given a week's vacation, because the years ahead will be very rigorous. It's a last chance to eat fine food, play sports, and just relax. They sent us to Bretagne. One day, we went swimming. We were going to jump from a cliff into the sea. I volunteered to go first, to show everyone what a sport I am. I jumped but I never came up. They waited and waited, and then went in after me. It seems that the water was much shallower than we guessed, and I damaged my back. I woke up in a Catholic clinic in a cast from my neck to my knees. I was there for months in a room with three other boys who couldn't move for one reason or another. All we could do was talk. One day, we were talking about Communism and one of the boys started to rant and rave, first about Communists, then about the wealthy class and then about Jews. I was very disturbed because the monks had taught us not to malign people, so I spoke up and told him we shouldn't be having this conversation. "Boy, you sound just like a Jew," he said.

That remark upset me terribly. What if I'm not a Christian, I thought. Not, what if I'm a Jew. That was not the problem. I was never anti-Semitic, and I never learned anything negative about Jews in school. I just couldn't get it out of my head. I decided to ask the priest who visited us on

Thursdays to hear our confession. I asked him, Father, is it possible I'm a Jew? He couldn't stop laughing. "You're in the top tier, one of our best students. Don't be ridiculous." I quieted down, but it still bothered me.

When it came time to take our vows, we went to Paris, where Cardinal Tisserant was going to give us a speech. Cardinal Tisserant was an outstanding humanitarian, very prominent in the time of Pius XII. I decided to ask him. "If he confirms that I'm not Jewish, case closed." The plan was, we were to receive our robe and crucifix, kiss the cardinal's ring, and go back to the bus. I don't know what possessed me but I kissed his ring, looked him in the eye, and said, "My name is Marcel Nakache and I have to know if it's possible that I'm Jewish."

He answered, "I know your mother, Rita. I saved her from the camps. She is Jewish and so are you."

Well, the world caved in. How could I now go on and be a priest if I wasn't even Catholic? I abandoned everything. The cardinal gave me my mother's address in Nice and told me to go to her. This was to be the first time I would actually live with her. She meant nothing to me in the sense that I didn't know her at all, but I was very aware that parents are to be respected, and I went. I didn't tell her that I had abandoned the Church because she was very religious and I didn't want to upset her. As best I could, I examined other religions, like Confucianism, but nothing spoke to me.

Unknown to me, Cardinal Tisserant contacted the chief rabbi of Nice, Rabbi Saltiel, and advised him to save me. Well, one day I opened the door and there is a very odd looking man—black beard, black clothes, very scary looking, really. He told my mother that he wants to care for me, and he told me privately that it does no good to deny who I am. I told him I couldn't possibly be Jewish because I'm not circumcised. He took me to Paris, where we went to the archives and found "David Nakache," my mother's father. The details matched my family history and I was convinced. I went back to Nice and told my mother I needed an operation. I didn't tell her what kind, but I had myself circumcised. By coincidence, Dr. Swillinger, the urologist who did the surgery, was also the community mohel [ritual circumciser].

I was enrolled in a study program with some Moroccan Jewish kids on their way to Israel. It was difficult for me. They were so strange—strange looking, strange customs, yelling during prayer and play. I was used to whispers. I learned about Shabbat and kosher food but I couldn't take the culture shock, so I ran away, back to my mother. She was thrilled to have me and cooked me my favorite meal every Thursday: ham in butter sauce. Well, by then I wasn't eating pig anymore because I knew Jews did not eat non-kosher food, but I couldn't hurt her feelings, so I was stuck. At least, though, I could buy kosher wine, which I did. She tasted it and declared it vile.

In January 1959, two months before my twentieth birthday, Rabbi Saltiel told me he would like to send me to Israel. For me, that was the Holy Land, the land of Jesus, Mary, and Joseph. I was thrilled to accept, without telling the rabbi the real reason for my joy. I sailed from Marseilles to Haifa. Haifa is a port city, built on a mountain. Lower Haifa is the industrial port area, and the residential district sits on the top half of the mountain, making the city famous for its breathtaking view of land and sea.

Once I arrived, I felt moved to recite a chaplet of thanks in a church, but the only Hebrew words I knew were "yes" and "no." I drew a picture of a church and showed it to a Christian Arab. He pointed up the mountain, and I saw a big white building with a gold dome but no cross. I thought maybe Israel doesn't put crosses on its churches. I walked up to the Upper City of Haifa and knocked on the door. The white-robed priest spoke French and explained that this was the Bahai Temple, no relation to Catholicism, but he pointed me in the direction of the nearest church, where I gave thanks for my journey. From there I planned to go to the contact Rabbi Saltiel had given me, but it turned out the address was outdated and the occupants had moved away. I was advised to go to a commune, where I could exchange work for room and board.

I went to Kibbutz Gesher, where they assigned me to the pigpen. I was shocked. I knew that pigs were the ultimate symbol of non-kosher food, and I couldn't understand what was going on. I lasted three days but I just couldn't take the thought of what I was doing. Not that the work itself bothered me. As an altar boy, my job at Christmastime was to stir the blood of slaughtered pigs so it wouldn't congeal.

I told Rabbi Saltiel I wanted to go back to France, but he said he had arranged for me to stay at Kibbutz Sde Eliyahu. I said, no, enough kibbutz. I was disappointed by the presence of pigs in a Jewish setting, but he said this was a religious kibbutz and he was certain I would fit in. He put me on a bus to Beit She'an, the closest town, and I got off in pouring rain and mud. It was late Friday afternoon with not a taxi in sight. Luckily, a bus driver spotted me and offered to drive me to within a quarter mile of the kibbutz. I thought he was crazy—what kind of halfway measure of help was this? As long as he's driving, why not take me all the way? I didn't understand that it would be inappropriate for him to drive all the way up to the gate of a religious kibbutz on the Sabbath.

When I walked through the gate, I heard singing. It was beautiful, and I walked in that direction. The dining room/synagogue was filled with light and people singing their Sabbath prayers. When I opened the door and they saw my muddy, bedraggled self, the singing stopped. I, to be polite, snatched off my head covering. Well, their jaws dropped even lower because that was the exact opposite of politeness in the company of people who wear skullcaps. A French-speaker named Michael Katz, who is today a close friend, put my cap back on and gave me a prayerbook. I had no idea which end was up because of the Hebrew, so I declined and took out my missal with the picture of Jesus with a big red heart on the cover. They were appalled, but I assured them that this was how I prayed.

A month passed and I still wanted to go home to France, but the kibbutzniks urged me to stay. Little by little I was integrated into religious life. I married a girl whose parents were cofounders of the kibbutz. They had no problem having a son-in-law who grew up thinking he was Catholic. We have five children.

Today I am an observant Jew. If you ask me what I believe, that is a complicated question. I'm a scientist. I see God under the microscope. I see Him in nature. Sometimes I take children on nature walks and we see snails and I say, yum yum! They ask me, can people eat snails? And I say, of course. They are a delicacy. And they ask, but aren't they non-kosher? And I say, yes, but I ate them before I knew I was Jewish. They look at me with amazement.

To this day, when the congregation is singing "Sim Shalom" in synagogue, I hear in my head the Latin version, "Dona nobis pacem." That happens with lots of prayers. They're singing in Hebrew, and I'm hearing a Catholic choir! Those seventeen years are part of me; the values and lessons were inculcated deep down.

In times of crisis, I pray like anyone else. First I ask God for help. If He doesn't answer, I ask the Devil. Somehow, between the two of them, things have always worked out for me!

Introduction

When the Landmann sisters were teenagers, their parents took them on a family trip to Germany.

When we entered Berlin, our father got so excited. "I lived here during the war," he said. And then, two blocks later, he said, "And here . . . And here." "How could you live in so many places?" we asked him. "Well," he said, "I only stayed a few days in each place." A lightbulb went off in my head. "Oh, so . . . you mean . . . you're Jewish? We're Jewish?" And my father looked at me and said, "Kind of . . . sure . . . of course." My feeling was, "Of course? Wait a minute . . ."

What is it like to find out you are not who you thought you were? Must you start recreating your self-image? What makes you who you are, your gene pool or your environment? I explored the answers to these questions by interviewing over 160 people who were raised as non-Jews, and at some point in their lives discovered they were of Jewish descent.

Perhaps it is our primal anxiety about identity that evoked such a strong reaction to the Madeleine Albright story. When Albright was named secretary of state, the *Washington Post* February 1997 coverage mentioned that her parents were Jewish refugees of wartime Czechoslovakia. Albright expressed shock that her parents had been Jewish. She claimed absolutely no prior knowledge. Her protestations produced widespread skepticism. How could a child of European parents have grown up with not a single question about their World War II experiences? And what child does not inquire after her grandparents?

Albright's denial elicited a storm of emotional responses in the media and in living rooms around the world. Reactions were vehemently polarized, ranging from cynical disbelief to heartfelt sympathy.

A large segment of the public said they could tell Albright was Jewish from day one—and if THEY could tell, then SHE should have known herself. Others said that even had she suspected, she could not possibly muster the psychological energy needed to challenge her parents' portrayal of the truth and risk their displeasure or distress. Following that line of thinking, one of the adoptees I interviewed said, "I understand Albright. If you challenge your parents, you lose your moorings. You're not in a position to make liars of them, so you repress the contradictions, and eventually your self-image wavers."

Shortly after the Albright profile was printed, diplomat Richard Holbrook's wife, journalist Kati Marton, came to their friend Madeleine's defense in a *Newsweek* article.[1] Marton had had a similar experience. While interviewing a Holocaust survivor in Marton's native Hungary, the survivor happened to mention that Marton's grandparents died in the Auschwitz death camp (as had Albright's maternal grandparents). This revelation took the twenty-nine-year-old Marton completely by surprise, and even when she confronted her parents, they were still reluctant to share their history, even though it was Marton's history, too.

Marton had been raised as a Catholic, and she had great difficulty understanding why her parents would have withheld defining information from her even after they arrived in America, where they were free to espouse any religious affiliation. She felt entitled to know the factual basis of who she was. Marton, like several of the interviewees in this book, concluded that Holocaust survivors cannot discount the possibility that being Jewish might one day again be dangerous.

"My parents must have thought they were protecting us." That is a litany often articulated by people who do not want to confront their parents' timidity or self-hatred, people awed by parents who survived despite impossible odds.

In July, nearly six months after the *Washington Post* profile, Albright visited the Old Jewish Cemetery of Prague and the Pinkas Synagogue, where she found the names of her paternal grandparents, Olga and Arnost Korbel, listed as victims of the Holocaust along with seventy-seven thousand other Czechs and Slovaks. The Jewish Telegraphic Agency quoted her Jewish tour guide as saying that she had clearly developed "very strong feelings about her Jewish roots."

This phenomenon of uncovering hidden roots fascinated me, and I determined to do some research. My curiosity had to do with people whose sense of self took a sharp, unexpected U-turn. I could have investigated other permutations of the discovery of fractured identity: finding out you are adopted, finding out your sister is your mother, finding out you are biracial, and so forth. But I was primarily interested in what it is like to find out you are of Jewish descent, probably because when I think of my own identity, I think "Jewish" before I think wife, mother, writer, American, or anything else.

Psychoanalyst Erik Erikson described identity as a "sense of being at one with oneself as one grows and develops, and a sense of affinity with a community's sense of being at one with its future, as well as its history or mythology."[2] In the ordinary course of identity formation, a person regards his parents as models and mimics their characteristics. If those characteristics eventually conflict with the child's peer group as he gets older, a crisis ensues. Historian Michael A. Meyer says that every Jew has a crisis of identity as soon as he matures enough to see the differences between Judaism and the surrounding non-Jewish world.[3]

But my focus for this project was a bit different. Rather than examining the discontinuity between family and society, I would be looking at the disruption that occurs when the familial identification changes retroactively. Simply put, what happens to your sense of self when you find out your parents are not who they said they were?

I placed both an author's query in the *New York Times Book Review* and postings on the Internet—on adoption webpages, religious websites, genealogy sites, anywhere and everywhere—seeking people raised as non-Jews who discovered they are of Jewish descent. Over a period of fifteen months, I was in contact with 178 individuals, 166 of whom I interviewed either in person, by telephone, or by mail. By definition, the people who responded are a self-selected group. They are literate enough to be reading the *Book Review* (forty-six letters, one phone call) and/or able to access the Internet. I located a few interviewees by word of mouth, often through siblings who had contacted me. Not everyone I interviewed was happy to have discovered his Jewish ancestry, so even self-selection did not automatically mean that the respondent had let out a whoop of joy at the news. But it did mean that the discovery had had a genuine impact on the person, enough to want to talk to me about it.

People find out in all sorts of ways about their family background. There are several dramatic scenarios among these interviews—deathbed confessions, drunken revelations, strangers showing up at funerals. Sometimes, just a slip of the tongue—often by a relative—provokes a confrontation. For Sarah Shoshana David, a form letter in the mail set her life on a completely different trajectory.

I was fourteen when Grandma Rose died. Three years later, a letter was forwarded to our house. Her brother Abraham, a ward of the state at Pilgrim State Psychiatric Hospital, needed consent of next of kin for surgery. Abraham Hoffman? Next of kin? Grandma always said she was an only child. Curious about this long-lost relative, my sister and I drove out to the psychiatric facility to meet this man claiming to be Grandma's youngest brother.

We walked into the day room at the hospital, and there was a man who looked exactly like Grandma. And also looked unmistakably Jewish. After a long conversation that mostly centered on his "remarkable" life story, I asked the obvious: Uncle Abraham, are you Jewish? "Aren't you?" he answered with a puzzled look. It's so trite that I hate to say it, but it's absolutely true: in that moment, huge inexplicable parts of my life made complete and overwhelming sense.

My incredibly Jewish-looking, Brooklyn-born grandmother, Rose, with her unmistakable accent, balabusta *[homemaker] cooking (matzo brei, kugel, stuffed peppers), and profound belief in education, learning, social justice, and* tzedukah *[charity] transmitted to me every bit of her lost culture, in every way but name only. I often think that we, her immediate family, were the only people who didn't realize she was Jewish. I was always puzzled by how she could ignore Christmas. And how shrimp, bacon, lobster, and clams were bad for her gall bladder.*

Rose had married her non-Jewish employer at the turn of the century. Her family pronounced her dead and never spoke to her again. She hid her Jewishness (but not very well, in retrospect) all her life after that. The family believes her husband also did not know.

I spent the next fifteen years in a quest for Jewish identity and Jewish knowledge. I moved to California, started a relationship with my beloved husband, and, shortly thereafter, began formal Jewish adult education. After several more years of study, a beit din [religious tribunal] of Conservative rabbis used the facilities at a local Orthodox shul to welcome me formally back to the congregation of Israel. It was not a conversion, but a rite of return, a ceremony that dates back to the times when the Marranos were forced to practice Christianity. So now, I have been for many years a fully practicing Jew. My identification with the Jewish world is so strong that I often forget the long path I had to take to come here. As my husband has said many times, he's always known I had a Jewish soul.

People frequently discover their background as a result of genealogy searches through census documents or ship manifests, church and synagogue records, even the telephone book. Sometimes a passport from the Old Country marked "Ivreii" or "Mosaiche" is the giveaway. Twenty-eight-year-old Frasier Collins had only to look in the mirror to know that he had a Jewish parent.

My mother, Carla, lived with Jake, but there was a month-long period when Carla and Jake separated. Carla was pregnant, but it was so early, she didn't know it. Carla started dating Chris and they had sex. (This was the sixties, time of free love.) The upshot was that Carla didn't really know who the father of her child (me) was. Jake offered to raise me, but she declined. That was in early 1968. Carla and Chris lived together for about a year. I was born and my mother moved us to another state. We lived with various relatives, including my grandmother in England for a while.

From the age of six and on, I spent my summers with Chris, who I thought was my [non-Jewish] father. So did he. Chris and Jake stayed friends. I remember at age sixteen or seventeen looking in the mirror and thinking, I look Jewish. I'm olive-skinned with dark, curly hair, green eyes, and a generous nose. By the time I turned eighteen, I looked exactly like Jake, who is Jewish. I mean exactly. There were times that Chris, Jake, and I would be together, and people would remark on how much Jake and I looked alike.

That same year, I was spending an evening with my mother and her husband. I was into punk rock then, wearing makeup and experimenting with drugs, staying up all night. My mother was a hippie, so these avenues of exploration didn't seem outlandish to me, but she apparently wanted to shock me into doing some soul-searching. It worked. Boy, did it work. She told me she was concerned about me, and then she segued into this revelation. She told me that Jake was my biological father, not Chris. She said she had decided she was never going to tell me, but she couldn't resist. To me that meant she always knew but wasn't going to tell. But she says she only knew for certain once I started looking so much like Jake.

I responded with emotional blackness. It was all so overwhelming. I moved back to Montana and signed up to take a music course with Jake. I didn't tell him what my mother had told me, even though she said the whole town knew except for Jake and Chris. Meanwhile, my mother wrote to an old friend in Montana saying, "I know you know all about this. Everyone does." So the friend went to Jake with it. Jake asked me and I admitted I knew. It had a huge impact on him. He has a son who looks a lot like me, and a daughter who looks a lot like my daughter.

Within a few weeks, Jake approached me and said he wanted to pursue genetic testing. We did. There was a 96 percent likelihood that Jake was my father, and zero percent that Chris could have been. I'm glad we did it. It gave me closure.

The fallout from Carla's revelation was shocking and painfully disruptive to Frasier, Chris, Jake, and their families. These are not their real names. This being a highly sensitive subject, more than a third of the respondents requested anonymity. Some do not want to be identified as Jews. Several have family members who do not want to be known as Jewish. Many have family members who do not know they are Jewish. A few carried my letter around with them for half a year or more until they gathered the courage to write. They said that the compulsion to speak out eventually overcame the angst of disclosure. On the other hand, four who have not resolved their own feelings about this unsettling development retracted their statements after we had had long talks about their backgrounds.

I heard from people in Eastern and Western Europe, Central America, Australia, New Zealand, and Israel, but by far the largest number of responses came from descendants of the two million Jews who immigrated to America between 1881 and 1920 to escape economic deprivation, political instability, and anti-Semitism. While most of these immigrants maintained, at least for a generation, their religious and cultural ties to Judaism (most settled, for example, in heavily Jewish enclaves like New York's Lower East Side), their children were often more interested in assimilating into American society than in maintaining their Jewishness. Indeed, because American society was especially receptive to Caucasian, upwardly mobile, second-generation Jews, it was relatively easy for people to hide their Jewishness, to reinvent themselves as nonreligious or as Christians. Sometimes Jewish origins simply fell away, forgotten in the absence of any serious obstacles to assimiliation.

Efforts to "fit in" could take an emotional toll, however. Psychologist Sue Finkelstein, for example, was born in 1929 to parents who had moved to the United States from Hungary after World War I, anxious to suppress their Jewish origins. Sue's father came from an intellectual family. He had been a mechanical engineer in Hungary but, unable to find employment in his field in America, he became a hairdresser, a compromise he found so shameful that he made his family lie about it. Sue's mother's family managed land tracts, and therefore identified with the landed gentry of Hungarian society. And with their anti-Semitism. When she left Hungary, Sue's mother also left behind every vestige of her Jewishness except, Sue recalls, that she always kept a box of matzo in the back of the kitchen cupboard, which she sometimes crumbled into her coffee. When Sue was eight, the family moved to the only Irish Catholic street in a Jewish section of the Bronx.

The other kids wouldn't play with me because I was a heathen. I had no religion. I was one of the three kids who showed up to school on Rosh HaShanah [Jewish New Year]. In eighth grade, when we lived in New Jersey, my parents started sending me to the Episcopal Church by myself on Sunday mornings. My mother and I were baptized. The night before the ceremony, my parents went to a party and that was the first time I saw my father so drunk he got sick. That was how he handled the baptism. He just couldn't stand up to my mother.

When I was belt high, I overheard a conversation in Hungarian among my father, his brother, and a friend. The memory is so clear that I can recall my father's pocket watch ringing in the middle of their talk.

My uncle said, "Well, whatever happens, I'm a Jew." I don't think I ever heard that word spoken in Hungarian before. I felt a huge stab of anxiety, but I covered it over. I figured out that they were discussing what they would do under Hitler, whether they would convert or hide. It's a very searing, forbidden memory, and I almost repressed it.

Years later, as a freshman at Douglass College, I realized that I had two sets of friends: nice WASPy girls from suburban New Jersey, and the daughters of central European Jewish intellectuals. I began to reflect on that. I felt enormously more at home with the Jewish girls. It was a cultural thing. They thought it was hysterical that I'd never seen a bagel. I didn't know the superficial stuff about being Jewish, but the ideas and principles mattered enormously.

I began to put things together and I finally pressed one of my cousins. He confessed that he was breaking an oath. He felt terrible about it, but I needed to know the truth. I was very shocked, even though I knew. You can't totally not know. You try hard to accept what you've been told but at the same time, your perceptions of these forbidden things are so highly charged that there's an anxiety level.

It's not as though the child doesn't process impressions. I was very anxious when I learned. After a while I became enraged. I was angry at the family conspiracy and furious with the lack of integrity. That's when all the anti-Semitic stuff rose up in me. I had assimilated that from my mother. Now I had to rethink my view of myself and of other people. I was envious that some people were absolutely clear about who they were and felt comfortable with it. That was not open to me. Not just the Jewish lie, but having to lie about my father's profession. Having to lie creates self-loathing.

And then there was my mother's craziness—her sense that she could present herself any way she wanted, and reality would bend to her will. There is something fundamentally not trustworthy about a parent who, for the sake of her own comfort, will deny a child some essential piece of information about who they all are. Once they bend reality, it's with respect to all kinds of things. As a normal person matures, he realizes his limitations. Not to realize them is an infantile kind of omnipotence. It was clear to me that their choice reflected a lack of integrity. Ironically, that perception saved me, because in reaction, I concluded that whatever it meant to be a Jew, I was one and needed to be.

Sue's account contains many of the elements common to this phenomenon of uncovered roots: suspicion of the truth, anger at compromised entitlement, anxiety over toxic secrecy, collusion among family members. Sue reversed her parents' rejection of their heritage and claimed that heritage as her own. But her pain and sense of betrayal at the hands of her parents suggests why, for some, the discovery of Jewish roots is at best a mixed blessing.

Nonetheless, Sue's reclamation of her Jewish heritage mirrors a growing trend in American society: the desire of people to investigate and discover who they are. The search may be for religious, ethnic, racial, or sexual identity, but in all cases the searcher is looking to develop or confirm personal identity within a larger (and presumably welcoming) community. As anthropologist Otto Maduro suggests, "there might be today in many circles in this country a positive predisposition to find in one's own possible Jewish roots a way to explain one's malaise at being *just anybody* in an anomic, anonymous place."[4] Historian Jonathan Sarna puts it succinctly: "It's 'in' to be Jewish now. People who are discovering they are Jewish are not hiding it."[5]

And yet the question remains: what does it mean to be Jewish? Does it mean you subscribe to monotheism and attend bar mitzvah celebrations? Is it eating bagels and voting Democrat? Buying Israel Bonds and crying at Holocaust commemorations? Does being Jewish mean you are of Jewish parentage? If so, which parent? My respondents included people who defined themselves as Jews if only their father was Jewish and people who identified as Jews if only their mother was Jewish, as well as people with two Jewish parents or with only distant Jewish ancestry.

In the view of the Jewish Reform movement, having one Jewish parent gives a child a presumption of Jewish descent, opening the potential for Jewish status to be conferred through "appropriate and timely public and formal acts of identification with the Jewish faith and people."[6] Orthodox and Conservative Judaism, basing their tenets on a Talmudic text,[7] define as Jewish anyone born to a Jewish mother and anyone who converts to Judaism according to Jewish law.

But the application of rabbinic law to real-life situations is not always so smooth. Sociologist Anselm Strauss asks, "If a gentile woman marries a Jew and embraces his faith, is she or is she not a Jewess? Suppose that she divorces him but continues to attend synagogue services regularly and raises her children as Jews, is she still Jewish? If he in turn grows unreligious and associates with fewer Jewish people than she does, who is the more Jewish . . . of the two?"[8]

Why, for that matter, is a convert to Judaism asked to commit to Jewish practice when a born Jew does not lose her status if she neglects or even renounces her Jewishness? And who gets to ask these questions? Is being Jewish a matter of self-selection? Are you Jewish if you so declare? Or do card-carrying members of the group have to meet the entry criteria of the leadership? More to the point, are you Jewish if you were raised as a non-Jew by parents who hid their Jewishness or were themselves ignorant of it?

Most intriguing for me is a question that emerged when I was deep into the interview phase. What do we learn about the concept of identity from those scores of people who said they were attracted to Judaism well before they discovered their Jewish ancestry? Fourteen of the individuals interviewed felt so strong a pull that they converted before they found out they had Jewish lineage. What is *that* all about?

The phenomenon of a sense of recognition recurred time and again in my conversations. Many people even used the same terminology: "a lightbulb went off in my head," "it spoke to me," "I felt comfortable with the belief system." People talked about finding resonance in the theology itself. Others spoke of feeling comfortable among Jews, or having a preponderance of Jewish friends. Several described finding Judaism as "coming home." "It was like looking in a mirror." To hear Sue Finkelstein tell it, "When I first started attending services, there were parts of the liturgy that moved me to tears in that 'pintele Yid' [tiny, inner Jew] sort of way. It was as though I had suddenly found some deeply buried home."

In the pages that follow are transcripts of my conversations with crypto-Jews (descendants of the Jewish victims of the Spanish Inquisition), hidden children of the Holocaust, children of Holocaust survivors, and adoptees. Rather than paraphrase, I have transcribed words as spoken. Where stream of consciousness obscured clarity, I have transposed sentences. The interviews are positioned between this introduction, which raises the questions I wanted to pursue, and the concluding chapter, which summarizes what I learned in answer to those questions.

Knowing who you are provides insulation against the onslaughts of a random universe. Sharing a common mission, common truth, and common history offers the comfort, even if it is imagined, of having a society of peers, an extended family. The impulse to find one's context, one's place in the galaxy is a basic need. That was the subtext to much of what I heard. These interviews give voice to that central element in the human soul.

Crypto-Jews

I remember grandmother taking me to what I thought was a church in Mexico City. We had to sit in the women's balcony in the back. There was a man leading the chants in a language I had never heard. I remember her saying, "Never forget who you are." I understand now that it was a synagogue. Later, when I asked my mother what my grandmother meant, she said it was a silly rumor and to put it out of my head. I couldn't, though.

For Jews the year 1492 recalls more than "Columbus sailed the ocean blue." It was the year of the Edict of Expulsion from Spain, the apex of the Inquisition, that period when the Jews of Spain and Portugal were given three choices: to convert to Catholicism, leave the Iberian Peninsula, or be killed. Those Jews who would not elect one of those three alternatives created a fourth: to live overtly as Catholics but covertly as crypto-Jews.

While most of the conversions to Catholicism resulted in absorption into the Catholic community, those converts who harbored or were suspected of harboring Jewish allegiance were killed, often at the stake. Many New Christians, as the converts were called, settled in Mexico, Central and Latin America, and the Caribbean. Those converts in Mexico who still practiced Judaism in secret were soon pursued by inquisitors sent from Spain to ferret them out. This time they fled north, to Texas, Colorado, and New Mexico. There they continued to live surreptitiously as Jews but outwardly as Catholics. In July 1997, more than five hundred years after the expulsion from Spain, I met some of their descendants.

The ultimatum to convert or die has been delivered to the Jew so many times that the Jewish response to the issue has become codified.

Jewish law requires its adherents to accept death rather than publicly renounce their faith. As a result, an implicit stigma attaches to those unwilling to offer themselves and their spouses and children as sacrifices to a belief. The descendants of the crypto-Jews are sensitive to that stigma.

The sensitivity over this tragic period in history plays itself out even in the nomenclature. It is inappropriate, for example, to refer to such a person as a Marrano, which, while it connotes a Jew who hid his Jewishness, actually means swine in Spanish. Marranos had to be more-Christian-than-Christian in order to escape suspicion, so they would make a show of eating the non-kosher pig. That is the less abrasive explanation for the use of the word. The other possible explanation for applying the word *Marrano* to Jews in a pejorative sense is because Jews were still reviled even after they converted.

More acceptable is the Hebrew word *anusim*, which means "those who were forced," referring to those Jews who converted under duress. *Converso* simply means "one who converted" and could denote a Jew who converted to Catholicism out of genuine commitment. Those who converted during the Inquisition either embraced their new religion to greater or lesser degree, or they retained Jewish customs sub rosa to the extent possible without being detected. Those latter are called "crypto-Jews."

One of the places I posted my query was on Sephardic (Spanish Jewish) Web sites. I soon learned that the seventh annual two-day conference of the Society for Crypto-Judaic Studies in Denver was imminent, and I made arrangements to attend. The conference started off with a modest cocktail party. There were small tables scattered about the hotel meeting room, with three or four participants seated at each. When I entered, the room was abuzz with people chatting away. I spotted an empty chair and sat down. We exchanged smiles around the table, and I listened as the two women and one man talked about a photo exhibit of Southwest American gravestones that had either Hebrew lettering or Jewish symbols etched on them. As soon as they reached a natural break in the conversation, the three turned to me.

"Are you here to research your genealogy?" one of the women asked.

"Not really. I'm a freelance writer doing a book on people who discover their hidden heritage. I thought this would be a perfect place to research that topic."

The only worse thing I could have said would have been that I was the Grand Inquisitor come from Ferdinand and Isabella's court. They looked at one another and sequentially excused themselves from the table. It was not until the end of the conference that I learned there had been a journalist at the previous year's gathering who masqueraded as a crypto-Jew (a crypto-crypto-Jew?) in order to gather material for a story. When people who had shared their history with him found out, they felt violated. The truth is, the crypto-Jewish community is very secretive and self-protective. Until I had listened to some of the presentations at the conference, I did not appreciate the fear many of the crypto-Jews still feel today. Once I did, I understood much better the tone of an electronic letter I received in May 1997, two months before the conference, from Maria B. Gonzalez.

Buenos Dias.

Are you sure you want to open this up to all Jews or are you most interested in Askenasim? You see, there are a lot of Sephardic conversos in this country and throughout Latin America and Spain. We can trace our Jewish roots through the most reliable form: the unaltered historical accounts passed down from generation to generation. We are told the truth only after we inquire and piece it together ourselves. The clues were always there; we just had to look.

Only recently have I disclosed my identity for the first time to a close friend. She has been so encouraging that it has given me the courage to approach you. I have, in the past, on many occasions been snubbed and outright rejected by the "white" Jews. That is why I ask if you are interested in including us as part of your research. Please don't feel obligated in any way. We have been living for the most part unaffected by the stereotypes imposed by "white" Jews.

Sincerely yours, Maria (A Catholic to my priest; a Jew to my rabbi.)

I was surprised and saddened by Maria's letter. Sephardic Jews, after all, are probably closer in ethnicity to the original Jews who left Egypt and received the Ten Commandments than am I, a blond, blue-eyed descendant of German (Ashkenazic) and Romanian Jews. I wrote back to Maria that I was most certainly interested in her heritage, and she requested that we speak by phone rather than communicate by mail. "I was trained to listen and observe subtleties by my grandmother," she said. She was skittish at the outset of our conversation, but as she relaxed, she became more discursive, and we ended up talking for quite a while.

I am descended from the Mendez family, believed to be originally from Madrid. There were several families who arrived onto the Mexican coast to the port of Tampico in the mid-1860s. Three of those families were related to one another: the names were Mendez, Vargas, Perez. According to the book entitled A History of the Marranos *by Cecil Roth, both Mendez and Perez are Sephardic Hebrew names. It was these three families who founded the town of Salem in Mexico. I've always wondered if that's related to Shalom or Salaam.*

We go back to fifteenth-century Spain and earlier. Some of us were exiled, some killed, some survived. Much of our history has been lost, but there are stories that were passed down by word of mouth. By the time I got to high school, I noticed that our family was different.

I was raised Catholic. I was baptized, went to church, got communion. My grandmother lived on a farm in Mexico. I stayed with her when I was a child. She had animals and would hire men to kill them when she needed meat. There was something special about the killing. She insisted that they kill them very fast so the animal would not suffer. Once it was killed, the animal had to be propped up by its hind legs until all the blood had drained into the ground, which I now know is related to Jewish kosher laws. To this day I cannot eat rare steak, it's so ingrained in me not to eat blood. In Mexico our family wasn't allowed to eat blood sausages, even though they are very popular. We never ate cheese and meat together, like everybody else. I thought it was just my grandmother's peculiarity. Now I know that Jews don't mix milk and meat. We were not allowed to eat the tail or hind part of the animal; it was considered filthy.[1]

Many of the kosher laws got confused because of the length of time they had to keep them repressed. Like, when visitors left, my grandmother would boil the pots and silverware. She had separate pots for each different kind of food. It was her attempt to keep kosher. They made me wash my hands a lot, especially before eating, like traditional Jews do. We never ate shellfish. Grandmother said it was because they were bottom feeders. We swept dirt to the middle of the floor instead of pushing it out the front door.[2] *Grandmother lit candles on Friday night. We never married outsiders, only second or third cousins and people from certain families, and the first-born son was always given the name of his father, making the name traceable for centuries.*

My mother was promised to the son of one of the other chosen families. Because she married someone else, she dishonored the family when she dishonored the agreement. They didn't want to accept me, but they did, on the condition that I would live with my grandmother and she would teach me the family customs. Our family reads between the lines about everything. There is a tremendous fear of discovery. I was shown a lot of the customs, but they were never explained. I don't think they knew they were Jewish customs. Anyway, we were so Catholic, you wouldn't believe it. We were almost obsessed with Catholicism.

When I made Jewish friends growing up, they kept asking me if I was Jewish. I remember in high school they showed us some concentration camp footage, and I felt like I'd been stabbed in the heart. That didn't happen with the Japanese internment films or the other war films. There was something about the Jews being killed that felt personal. I had never felt a pain like that. I've never told this to anyone. I've thought about it a lot. Maybe there is something transmitted genetically. I've always felt a comfort level around Jews that I couldn't understand.

Finally, many years later, I felt compelled to find out why I was so different. I talked to a Sephardic rabbi who pieced my story together. He looked like me, he talked like me. In Mexico, when amongst ourselves, my family spoke some words and phrases that are an ancient form of Spanish. They also spoke some Catalan. When that rabbi spoke Ladino [Hebraic Spanish], I was able to understand him. The more I knew, the more I wanted to know. I even went to Spain and found the areas my family fled to when they left Madrid. I found the village my mother's family came from in Catalonia, north of Barcelona.

My cousins don't want to know about our heritage and my mother considers it ancient history. The only thing they have preserved of Judaism besides the customs is the belief that there is only one God, and that Jesus was a son of God but not God himself. That's a big difference from Christianity, which believes that Jesus was divine.

When my friends would ask if I'm Jewish, I would say "no," because Judaism is a religion and I wasn't raised a Jew. I don't talk about my background much. I can't explain the fear, but it's almost like an instinct. It was very scary to find out I belong to people who were persecuted, but I'm also curious. I want to learn about Judaism, but at my own pace. I've learned some good things from Catholicism and from Judaism. I can't say which I would choose.

Maria's recital of her history contains many of the components described by anthropology professor Seth Kunin.[3] Kunin divides the crypto-Jewish community into four categories: (1) people who practice Jewish rituals, self-identify as Jews, and hold Jewish beliefs (such as monotheism); (2) people who have been told or have discovered through genealogy searches that they are Jewish; (3) people with Jewish customs in their family, but who consider themselves non-Jews; and (4) people who have none of the three criteria (practice, identity, beliefs), but feel themselves to be Jewish.

In a discussion of whether Jewishness is an attained or an ascribed status, crypto-Jews offer a fascinating model. Those crypto-Jews who are told by their parents that the family is Jewish, or discover as much when they research their roots, are defining themselves genealogically (by descent). Those who identify as Jews on the basis of their customs or beliefs, or simply by virtue of "feeling Jewish" would fall into the "consent" category. And to ratchet the complexity up a notch, it is worth noting that the two often overlap, for instance, in people who discover their Jewish lineage and then figure out retroactively that the family emphasis on the Ten Commandments was Jewish as well.

I was glad that Maria opened up during our conversation, and it was not until two months later at the conference that I appreciated just how much of an effort it must have taken for her to do so. The opening conference remarks were delivered by Esmeralda T., a fortyish woman with very straight dark hair, a tailored pants suit, and no-nonsense shoes that matched her demeanor. She ascended to the podium with an assertive stride, a stride that announced her intensity.

I participate in crypto-Judaic matters despite the jeopardy it puts my family in. I don't reveal details about our background, but I know that people like myself need guidance and I am committed to give them whatever help I can, just as I have been helped to recover my genealogy.

She went on to read a letter from a woman desperate to find relatives, her aunt having contracted a Jewish genetic blood disease. That disease was the first clue the family had of its Jewish ancestry. Toward the end of the emotional letter, Esmeralda broke down in tears. "This is why I do what I do," she said in conclusion, unable to continue.

I still had difficulty absorbing the idea of actual danger befalling people who revealed their Jewish heritage, but it became clearer the following day, when Margarita Hernandez read some of her poetry on the subject of recapturing lost identity. I recognized her as one of the women who had left the table two nights before when I introduced myself. She had a striking appearance—a pale white complexion, contrasted by black hair and deep plum lipstick. To introduce her work, she talked about her life. Even her prose had the dreamy quality of poetry.

My family has lived in an adobe house in New Mexico since 1850. My mother is Presbyterian. My father is a pseudo-Catholic. His credo is the Ten Commandments. We were raised differently than our neighbors. Why? Who am I? Why am I different?

I have two sisters and a brother. Three years ago we began to discover our Jewish identity. Now what? We have three problems. First of all, three of us felt the urge to pursue our heritage, and the fourth remains a fundamentalist Christian. We don't want this new information to create a family rift.

Second, imagine what happens to a person who announces his Jewishness at work. It can be very difficult, to say the least. I was interviewing for a job two weeks ago. When the personnel director looked at my résumé, she asked, why do you belong to so many Jewish groups? I didn't get the job.

Third, how many Hispanos are prepared to self-declare? You become an oddity.

I look at the landscape of horizon, cactus, sky, and I wonder—who am I? Where am I going? Why did my people come here? How do I tell others and whom do I tell? Why should I give an interview to a stranger who knows nothing about me? Nothing about us?

Among the conference presenters was David Gitlitz, who delivered a historical overview of the period.[3] Gitlitz cited a fascinating statistic, that almost everyone of Spanish or Portuguese descent is likely to have some Jewish ancestry. Nevertheless, he cautioned that there are significant difficulties in tracing a clear line of crypto-Jewish roots. For one thing, Gitlitz has little faith in the use of surnames as an indicator because Jews had to discard typically Jewish names in order to escape suspicion or persecution. Furthermore, with no Jewish models to learn from, no books or artifacts, the transmission of Judaism suffered. Being Jewish became more a matter of intent than action.

There has been so much interaction over the centuries with the surrounding non-Jewish community, and so much variation in beliefs and customs that the legitimacy of crypto-Judaism is clouded. After centuries of intermarriage and cultural assimilation, how can anyone be sure that crypto-Jews are descended from Jewish ancestors in an unbroken chain? Add to that a motif of self-imposed secrecy, even between parents and children, and the problem is compounded. If parents were afraid to follow Jewish practices or tell their children the family is Jewish, how Jewish can the family remain, especially through the generations? Doubts about their authenticity make their reentry into the Jewish mainstream a challenging proposition.

The issue of legitimacy is laced with bitterness. Today's crypto-Jewish descendants' pride is injured when their heritage is viewed as suspect. After all the pain our ancestors suffered at the hands of the Catholic Church, they protest, we now have to endure the suspicion of our own people?

As I was rushing out of the final conference session to catch my plane home, an attractive silver-haired woman with cornflower blue eyes tugged at my sleeve and whispered, "I'm Miriam." I tried hard to place her but she could see from my befuddled look that I could not. "I sent you an email." I still did not know who she was. "Ah! Miriam! I'm so glad you introduced yourself. Thank you. I'm sorry that I have to run, but it's wonderful to meet you." I looked up her correspondence when I got home. And I really was glad that she introduced herself.

When I was twelve years old, my grandfather, George Ramus (originally Ramos), told me that he was an English Sephardic Jew. It made quite an impression on me. In college I took a course in Judaism given by a rabbi. It explained many things to me. I was raised Catholic but when I was about twenty-nine years old, I decided I could not be Catholic anymore. I always felt as if I didn't quite belong in Catholicism or Christianity.

Recently I have been researching my grandfather's genealogical roots, and have been visiting a Sephardic synagogue. I enjoy the service and feel stirred in my heart.

Last January I changed my name from Mary Wagoner to Miriam Ramos. My husband, Richard, goes to synagogue with me and is very supportive.

I believe I inherited "tissue memory" or genes from this side of my family. I have many interests and traits similar to my grandfather's family. I sincerely identify with my Jewish roots. I honor and revere them; but I just don't know what I will do at this point. I guess I will continue to reflect on this and read the different books I have collected on Judaism.

This is about all. I didn't expect to write this much.

Sincerely, Miriam Ramos.

I wrote back to Miriam after the conference and she shared more details with me about her grandfather, details that were not possibly but definitely Jewish.

I was raised Roman Catholic, as was my mother and her mother, my grandfather's wife. When I was twelve, I saw my grandfather facing the window, hand on head and speaking softly in a foreign language. In reply to my question, he told me it was Hebrew and that he was praying. I asked him why and he responded, "Because I'm a Jew!" I ran home to my mother and announced that Grandpa was Jewish. She didn't seem amazed and cautioned me not to tell anyone just then.

Grandpa's dishes were kept separate from ours. He never ate pork, and when I asked about it, I was told "Grandpa doesn't like it." The answer was curt and I knew, in my child's way, that there was more to it.

My grandfather never criticized Catholicism nor emphasized his being Jewish for the remaining eight years I knew him. He was a fine, moral, soft-spoken man, whose honesty and reliability was never questioned. The more I looked at photos, read his poetry, thought of him and the events in his life, the stories he told me about his own family, their interests, values, and artistry, the more I recognized my genetic heritage. I cherish the knowledge that I am part Jewish.

Another person who became more expansive with me after the conference was the poet Margarita Hernandez, whom I telephoned a few weeks following my return. Although it has been five years since she discovered her roots, Margarita is still enthusiastic about her find. I shared with her my initial confusion at the reluctance of crypto-Jews to "come out." She told me that even though she writes newspaper articles about her history, she is still anxious.

We're not accepted. One of my dad's relatives had his headstone burnt. And when we wandered onto some property that used to belong to my dad, the current owner shooed us off. I thought he might have been about to pull a gun on us. There was a definite atmosphere of danger and imminent physical harm. We were known to be "different," and if they had realized exactly why, it would have been a lot worse.

We had customs that were unlike our neighbors'. My grandmother would throw an egg in the garbage if it had a blood spot in the yolk, which I now know is a kosher law. We would burn our fingernail clippings in the stove, another Jewish law. Around Passover, during Semana Santa [Holy Week], we would eat quelites [lambsquarters], and we would have a special meal. During the year, when we baked bread, we would take off a piece and burn it—another Jewish practice. And for forty days after childbirth, women were considered unapproachable. Now that's straight out of the Pentateuch! It blew me away when I realized that!

Growing up, we didn't go to church. Our parents sent us to a nondenominational school whose foundation was the Ten Commandments and good deeds. When I was in junior high, the civil rights movement was in full swing, and I remember telling my grandfather proudly, "We're Chicanos." He was a very mild man. I never saw him angry or upset, but he was that day. He took down his father's Spanish-language journal from 1893, and showed it to me. "We're Spaniards. Never forget." I had seen the journal before, but this time it was pivotal for me. I started to do research and by my early twenties I had traced our family back to Cordoba and Medina.

Five years ago, our family gathered for a wedding. By then my suspi-

cions were very strong. I had done a lot of reading on the Jews of New Spain and I decided I must tell my siblings. Well, my sister's reaction was, "Are you just figuring that out now? Haven't you thought about the way we grew up? In high school, my Spanish teacher asked where we're from. I told her we're from northern New Mexico. She said, 'You're one of those Sephardic Jews who ran away with Columbus.'" My sister couldn't believe how slow I was in realizing our connection. She continued, "I remember drawing a picture of the Morada, the Catholic chapel. I drew a crucifix and, I don't know why, but I also drew a Star of David. When Mom saw it, she said, 'You shouldn't draw that. It's the holy symbol.'"

My brother's reaction just shocked me to pieces. He opened the top button of his shirt and showed me his Star of David necklace! He said he hadn't felt Hispanic since eighth grade. And he told me he had studied everything he could get his hands on about the Holocaust.

When I talked to my aunt, she said, "Oh, honey, we know, but we've been Catholic so long." There's a lot of family discomfort around this subject. Nobody wants to invite social ostracism. Many family members belong to the Penitentes group. It's an offshoot of the Catholic Church, supposedly. When a person dies, for example, they have a brotherhood that washes the body and wraps it in white linen. They bury it in a pine box. The night before the burial, the brotherhood (or sisterhood, if it's a woman) holds a vigil until the funeral. All of that is exactly in keeping with Jewish tradition.

It's sad that my siblings and I hadn't spoken of this until we were in our forties. It was such a healing moment. It was like there had been a hole inside us. It's taken me a long time, but now I see things more clearly. It's like there's a genetic coding.

The Denver conference was primarily academic. When I returned home and resumed my interviews, their tone reverted to the more personal. One of the warmest, most cheerful correspondences I had was with Rogelio B. Amaral, who was very generous in his use of exclamation points and romantic reminiscences. After the first few paragraphs, I pictured him as a mustachioed Latin lover, and my inner ear heard his letters in a Spanish accent. I had seen his posting on the Internet indicating that he was researching his background, so I wrote to him offering some genealogy Web sites that might be helpful.

Hello, Barbara! My name is Rogelio B. Amaral. I run an orphanage with twenty-one kids from an Austrian institution called SOS Kinderdorf International. My mother's maiden name was Elena Barragan. I just discovered that my mother's family came from a Sephardi family of conversos established in San Luis Potosi, Mexico, in the late sixteenth century. All I know is that her family originally came from Toledo, Spain.

Most of my family have been raised as Christians, but our names are Jewish! Abraham, Isaiah, Zacarias, Elias; and all the women in our family are given names like Sarah, Ruth, Miriam, Isabel, etc. My father, against my mother's wishes, gave the name Rogelio to me. She had chosen the name Jared. Many of our celebrations coincide with Jewish holidays. Uncle Abraham always killed a tender goat called "cabrito" during the Easter festivities. He said it was to commemorate when the Patriarch was ordered to kill his eldest son and ended up offering a tenderling instead. The knife was blessed before the killing and the meat was cut with precision. (Now I know about the kosher laws.) I wondered what was the meaning of that and asked around. The neighbors told me my uncle was a little nutty. Ha, ha. Now I know!! Another thing: we do not eat pork. No Sir! And: all of our men are circumcised. My mother never explained to me why. She just told me it was for practical purposes. (I still wonder what she meant by "practical," ha, ha!!)

I feel very comfortable thinking about myself as a Jew, although I am not religious at all. This might be the only reason that has kept me from making the alijah [move] to Israel. I don't know what to do about that. At fifty-one, it may not be a very wise move to think about going to Israel. And being a secular Jew is not very well recommended there nowadays, ha, ha . . . After receiving your letter, I would like to make contact with you because I'm really interested in finding my origins. My aunts and uncles are dead, and my cousins don't care about this, really. Half of them are Catholic, the rest left that faith and went to the Protestant (Pentecostal) side.

I wrote back to Rogelio asking him how he discovered his mother's Sephardic background. Was it surprising?

Hello Barbara!

Shalom aleijem! Five years ago, when I was the principal in a high school run by the Salesian order, a Catholic priest named Juan de la Fuente Burton told me if I knew the origin of my mother's last name, Barragan. I told him I knew it was from Aragon in Spain. He laughed when he told me that I was far from my site of origin. He told me about the expulsion and about Toledo, the place he said was the real location of my family's origin. He told me he knew my grandfather and most of the Barragans in the region. In his opinion they were all conversos. I thought about my mother's physical appearance—the curly hair, the nose . . . it was so obvious!!! It was like a spark. Like if a curtain opened and a whole scenario appeared in front of me. There we were, after so many years since the moment of departure from our beloved "Sepharad." Yet, I don't regret our Christianity, because Jesus was a Jew after all! Ha, ha . . . and there we were mixing both legacies, which I embrace proudly. What is your opinion about this, Barbara? Could I be a true Sefardi Jew? Ha, ha . . .

Hugs, Rogelio Amaral

I told Rogelio his letters were fascinating and I thanked him for being so open. I asked him whether he had been a religious Catholic beforehand.

Yes, I was. I met Father de la Fuente in the Seminary. I was bound to be a Salesian priest, provided I finished my studies. I left the seminary because of two reasons: First, because of a lovely girl called Carmen . . . ha, ha . . . Second, because of my recently discovered Jewishness. When Father Burton told me about my Jewish background, it felt as natural as could be. All the pieces fell into place. You see what I'm talking about? Eventually I became an agnostic.

Rogelio's correspondence with me was lighthearted in tone, but not at all lightweight. I took very seriously every detail people shared. I regarded their revelations as a sacred trust, and so, when Joe Zavala contacted me with his startling story, I tried hard to understand his mindset, much as I was inclined to be skeptical. He spoke in a deep voice with a Texas twang, and needed no prompting.

My dad comes from a Spanish family on his father's side. There was bad blood between my father and his mother. They didn't talk for years, until she was on her deathbed.

Our family name was originally de Zavala. I found out we have roots in Montenegro, in the Yugoslav Republic. The family went from Yugoslavia to Spain. De Zavala is also a prominent name in Texas. Lorenzo de Zavala, originally from Mexico, was the first vice president of the Republic of Texas.

I always favored Jews. As a kid I wanted to go to summer camp with my Jewish friends. My grandfather died when my dad was young, and a lot of customs in the family were lost. My dad was brought up Catholic. From my recent studies, I figured out why: the Spanish Inquisition.

The Zavalas are believers in Christ. I was worship leader at our base chapel in Germany. We go wherever God leads us. Nine months ago, God spoke to me and said, find a Messianic congregation.[5] *So one Friday night I went. The rabbi-pastor said, "Hey, I've done a study of Sephardic Jews, and Zavala is a very Jewish name. It's from the Hebrew: gold of God." When I told my dad, he said, "Oh yeah? So where's all our money?"*

I was shocked to hear about the Jewish connection. It was a real bombshell. Now I had a struggle. What do I do? Do I follow a new path? Or stay what I am? Then God spoke to me again. Be yourself, He said. That gave me peace of mind. I've been studying Messianic Judaism ever since, and when I have a question, I ask our rabbi-pastor. Some of the Jewish traditions give me problems, but then I look into them and find a resolution. My rabbi-pastor told me, "You're fulfilling a prophecy of the dispersed coming back together. You're finding lost Jews and bringing them back."

Some months later, I wrote to Joe about a Web site that mentioned Zavala as a crypto-Jewish name, and he wrote back to say that he had found some possible Jewish ancestry on his mother's side of the family. The last thing he wrote was, "Take care and be blessed," which I heartily reciprocated.

Fifty-two-year-old Charlene Neely saw my posting on the Kulanu website. Kulanu (Hebrew for "all of us") is an American organization that studies and maintains contact with Jewish descendants from Portugal and Spain. Unlike Joe Zavala, who sought to combine his dual heritages, Charlene chose between the two.

Having converted to Judaism as a teenager, decades before she discovered her Jewish roots, Charlene gives the sense of being entirely comfortable with her identity. She did not regard her discovery as a form of validation, because she already felt legitimately Jewish. But she has used it as a tool to convince Jews to be proud of their heritage.

I was born in L.A., but we moved to San Diego when I was five. My father is from Cornwall, England, and my mother's was among the first thirteen families to settle New Mexico. They were from Gallegos in Galician northern Spain. We had an Old World value system, a strong sense of being part of an ethnic group. But things were not so wonderful in California if you were Hispanic. I remember hearing my parents talk about a petition against them when they wanted to build a house in Long Beach, because the neighbors thought my mother was Mexican. I grew up aware of that prejudice.

Neither of my parents was Jewish. My father was a non-practicing Protestant, and my mother was from a strong Catholic family. When she married out of the faith, the Church tossed her out. We didn't have any religion in the house except that my mother expressed a strong feeling of one God. Jesus was never part of it. She taught us to do good to our fellow human beings, and she stressed education. Of twenty-nine cousins, I'm the only girl with a college degree.

At thirteen, I felt there was a spiritual hole in my life. I started asking my friends if I could go to services with them. I went to all kinds, but each felt uncomfortable because I didn't believe in Jesus. It made no sense to me, and I was brought up not to close my mind.

At the beginning of sophomore year, my mother said, why not ask Susie to take you to synagogue? Susie's response was, "Are you out of your mind?" as if to say, why would anyone in their right mind want to be Jewish if they didn't have to? But the minute I walked in, it was like, holy smokes. This was home. This was people caring about each other, welcoming each other, hugging! Imagine a church: you walk in, you shut up, and you pray. Our problem as Jews is, you walk into the synagogue and you never stop talking! The pronouns in the service struck me, too. Christian prayer has to do with the singular: MY *personal salvation. "I" and "me" are all over the service. In the synagogue, everything was "our" and "we." There was a sense of community, responsibility. And family was predominantly part of Jewish theology and life. You're not alone.*

I went to talk to the rabbi. So did my parents. I started meeting with him weekly. I even went to confirmation class with kids my age. I studied all sophomore year, and in June, at age fifteen, I converted.

When I got married, my mother's mother danced with the rabbi. She laughed and said, "Maybe I'm Jewish, too." I thought, wow, how supportive. I became a Jewish educator, very involved in the Jewish community. When my younger son had to do a family tree for school, we researched the archives on my mother's side. We went back four hundred years, and found a relative who came to the New World in 1541. We found names like David, Daniel, Abram, Jakovo. My mother's family tree was more like a bush! So much inbreeding. It was mind-blowing. She and I are third cousins. Everyone within ninety miles is a cousin. We have a complete organ donor strip in New Mexico!

When I read [New Mexico's state historian] Dr. Stanley Hordes's articles on crypto-Jews, I was engulfed by the implications. It's not like there was one "smoking mezuzah," but there were lots of little clues. Some I came on simply by asking my mother questions. Just last year she mentioned that her family never ate pork. She thought it was because it was too expensive. Her mother lit candles in the bedroom every Friday night. I thought it was a Catholic thing. I never connected it to my Shabbat candles until I read Hordes.

It's a big responsibility: five hundred years and now I find myself home. There are layers of Catholicism over the Judaism, and when you become Jewish you have to set them aside, which is difficult, because those layers are what kept you alive for five centuries.

I dislike when converts are called "Jews by choice." What are born Jews? Jews-by-force? It's important to me that people realize: if you become Jewish, you have to do it in its totality. It's hard enough being accepted by the Jewish community when you convert. You can't make a half-hearted commitment and expect to be welcomed.

There's something intrinsically powerful about Judaism. Finding my roots doesn't make me feel more Jewish. I'm glad I converted long before I discovered my background. The only reason I tell my story is so Jews won't turn their backs on converts who marry in. On the one hand, the

Jewish community alienates them, and on the other, they bemoan the intermarriage rate. Hey, why not try to kill yourself twice?! Be sensitive to the intrinsic value of Judaism. That's my message. Let's not shortchange who we are. You can be away five hundred years and then come home.

The same sense of a fevered search that I observed at the conference of the Society for Crypto-Judaic Studies exists on the discussion group Anusim, the busiest of all my email subscriptions. Every day I open my program to find a multitude of letters describing family names or rituals, and asking whether these could be evidence of a crypto-Jewish past. Speaking at the conference, psychiatrist David Kazazz said he founded the Resource Center for Crypto-Jews with Seth Ward of the Center for Judaic Studies at the University of Denver, for people engaged in a search. He sympathized with their need for completeness. He noted that the issue of personal research is not exclusive to Jews or adoptees but to anyone with a truncated sense of self. "They could be Gypsies, they could be anything. But they need to know who they are." The center gets one or two calls each week from people asking whether they might be descended from conversos.

Nan Rubin, project director of the documentary *Hidden Jews of New Mexico,* says National Public Radio was inundated by phone calls after its 1987 broadcast of "Search for the Buried Past." That twelve-minute piece, which was repeated in 1992, elicited the most mail NPR had ever received to date. According to Rubin, people think of crypto-Jews as exotics huddled in an adobe, waiting to be Judaized. The real reason these stories resonate is not because they are romanticized, she says, but because "people are drawn to identity issues."

Not all the crypto-Jews I interviewed live in the southwest United States. The others were equally intent on locating their roots and establishing their identity, but with a major difference—the crypto-Jewish descendants in places other than the American Southwest were not wrapped in that mantle of fear. Perhaps because their grandparents had not been hunted down in Mexico, or because they did not live in overwhelmingly Catholic communities, these others spoke more freely about their newly discovered past.

Unlike the people I met at the Crypto-Judaic Studies conference, Sophia's family hailed from Sicily, one of the havens temporarily opened to Jews fleeing the Spanish Inquisition. I had called Sophia, a fifty-year-old professor of philosophy, in May 1997, when the rabbi who converted her to Judaism gave me her name. While I was in Denver meeting crypto-Jews, Sophia was in Italy meeting her cousins for the first time. When I spoke to her in May, she was preparing for that trip.

My parents are American-born. My mother's parents are from Sicily, my father's mother is a New Yorker, and my father's father is from Florence. I was sent to Catholic school, but my parents never went to church, which at the time I thought was hypocritical.

I met my husband in 1975, but we didn't get serious until three years later. His parents are Jewish, but, as good Trotskyites, brought him up with absolutely no religion. On Passover, for example, they had no Seder, but they'd eat matzo balls with their dinner. That was it. In 1978, he started thinking about religion. He decided he wanted me to become Jewish so our kids would be Jewish. That was fine with me. He didn't really believe in God so it wasn't as though I had to commit to much of anything. We took a twelve-week course at Hebrew Union College, and decided to join a Reconstructionist temple. The rabbi got to know me and felt I would find a Conservative conversion more meaningful, so I went to study with Rabbi Stephen Lerner. We developed a very special relationship. We're both academics, so we had many fascinating conversations. The four classes I took with him were more anecdotal than rigorous, though he assigned me reading material. He had me light Friday night candles, eat kosher meat, things like that. In the back of my mind, I was thinking: my grandmother used to do these things—soak meat in salted water, broil steak on a separate grill, refuse to eat seafood.

My mother was a very busy woman, so I practically lived with my grandparents. They spoke Italian but understood English. They called me their daughter, not their granddaughter. Grandmother used to pull the shades down on Friday night and light candles in front of statues of saints. I remember her striking the match and telling me, "this is for after you pull the shades." When I learned about Shabbat candles, it was like a light went off in my head. She was very old when she met my husband. "Is he Jewish? Okay." I even remember her teaching me to sweep toward the middle of the room, like crypto-Jews did.

Grandmother's name was Annamaria. She came from Castelbuono, a town of refuge in 1492. Jews were given an extra year to stay there. All the names in Castelbuono are Anna. I have cousins named Anna. My mother's name is Annette. I'm going there this summer to look at tombstones and read church records. There has always been a priest in my family.[6] *Grandmother said our women had to marry within the family, and the priest would tell them whom to marry. She herself married out of the family. She got away with it because she was her father's favorite. Grandfather worked for her father, and they fell in love. Besides, her father had already "given" a daughter to the family, so that made it easier for her to marry out.*

When I converted to Judaism, I felt as if I'd never been anything else. My husband and I are very active in our synagogue now. Our parents have been very supportive. We have a big Seder every Passover. I feel my life has brought me to a position where I can interpret all these items that by themselves don't signify anything but when they are added up paint a picture. I feel I've received a message: Nobody said kaddish *[the Jewish mourner's prayer] for this family for five hundred years. This will be my project. I'm going to find a way to memorialize them.*

At summer's end, I wrote to Sophia to ask how her trip had been.

I'm going back in January to see my new family again. I met more than one hundred people I'm related to. My grandmother is a legendary figure in the family for her beauty, kindness, gentleness, and love for my grandfather, which is exactly how I remember her. Everything was as she said, only better—I couldn't have even imagined it.

Unfortunately, the church and castle where the records are kept were closed for renovation. I learned a great deal, though, about family surnames and customs, and am even more convinced that the family was crypto-Jewish.

The Jamaicans I spoke with fit more into the category of people who "feel Jewish." Small wonder, considering Jamaica's eclectic Jewish history. In *The Secret Jews*, Joachim Prinz describes Jamaican crypto-Jewry in a section on international commerce.

> Others settled in the West Indian archipelago and became deeply involved in the newly developing sugar trade. In the seventeenth century the European settlers, on the island of Barbados, were mainly Marranos who had emigrated from Holland after converting to Judaism . . . In British Jamaica, the Jews were active in the cultivation and refining of sugar, and they were so valuable to the economy that when some Christian merchants asked the governor in 1681 to exclude the Jews, their petition was rejected.[7]

In successive centuries, Jews arrived from both Sephardic (Brazil, Curacao) and Ashkenazic (Bordeaux, Bayonne, Amsterdam) communities. There was considerable intermarriage, such that a large percentage of the Jamaican population is thought to have Jewish ancestry. The possibility is strong; the certainty is elusive.

Physician Anthony Leigh MacFarlane lives in Canada now, but his baritone has retained a trace of its Jamaican musicality, those liquid *l*s and the drawn-out "ah" sound for *a*: Jah-may-kah. Tony showed me a photo of his father. But for the intervening years, they could be identical twins. Those are strong genes. And the picture of his father's Jewish mother showed what could have been a fraternal twin, so alike are the features. All three share a café-au-lait complexion, wide nose, curly gray hair, eyes that home in on their target with an encompassing intelligence. As we walked to the subway, Tony maneuvered himself to the street side of the sidewalk in a chivalrous gesture that I have not seen in decades. A gentleman and a gentle man, in speech and action.

My father was the illegitimate son of Alexander MacFarlane and Agatha Mendes, my Jewish grandmother. MacFarlane's wife was sick. He was going to marry Agatha after his wife died, but he himself died soon after. People used to tell me my grandmother was Jewish, but I had no idea what it meant. I asked my non-Jewish grandmother and she said, "The Jews are a proud, stiff-necked people." The tone of the message said: This subject is taboo and they are not nice people.

Jamaica is a plantation society. It was very structured. The owner was the absolute boss. Then there were house slaves, field slaves, and intermediate functionaries. That's why even today, it's difficult to get certain kinds of information. Jamaicans are bred with a need to keep secrets.

Slaves didn't want the masters to know what they were doing, and the master didn't want the slaves to acquire knowledge. That's the background you need to understand my family history.

My grandmother paid for my education, something she highly valued. I was taught by Jesuits. They discouraged me from pursuing higher education, but by 1957, I was in university. Two years later, I came to Canada for a ten-week vacation. At that time I was a practicing Roman Catholic. I figured I'd spend some time in New York before going back to school. I traveled by bus, and this one time I sat next to a guy who started chatting. After fifteen minutes we exchanged names.

"I'm Irving Goldstein."

"What kind of name is that?"

"I'm Jewish."

"Jewish? My grandmother was Jewish. What's a Jew?"

When I got back to Hamilton, I ran into a girl I knew. She said, "What did you do this summer?" I said, "I met a Jew." She said, "Big deal. I'm Jewish, too. Want to come to synagogue with me?"

I went and soon realized I was much more comfortable in the synagogue than I ever was in a church. I received a lot of dinner invitations and was exposed to highly intellectual conversation. One day I took a look at the Encyclopedia Judaica. *There were six pages on the Mendes family. That was my validation. It was the first time I heard the word Sephardic. I started reading like crazy:* Exodus, *William Shirer,* The Last of the Just. *It's in the blood. I can't otherwise explain my drive to know my background.*

Just before it came time for me to go back to Jamaica, I asked the rabbi to convert me, which he did. After my medical training, I established a practice in Canada. Today I am president of the Reform congregation I belong to.

When I was about nine, on the plantation, I read a book about a royal child who was substituted for a commoner, his exact look-alike. Mark Twain was it? I always felt different when I was at the Jesuit school. I used to put that down to the fact that I came from the "country." I experienced a strong conviction that I was in the wrong place, that I wasn't recognized as who I should be. I have since learned that this is a common phenomenon among children, but with the reconnection to my Spanish-Portuguese roots, I had the distinct feeling that I had come into my true identity.

The authenticity of crypto-Jews was not my focus; my concern was the experiences and reactions of those individuals who discovered or suspected they were descended from Jewish victims of the Inquisition. They were tenacious in their quest to establish their identity. Once they made the connection to the past, the experience of their forefathers was very real and meaningful to them. How they got to that understanding—whether through culture, genealogy, or inner drive (consent or descent)—made little difference to them. What mattered was knowing who they were and where they came from.

Hidden Children

When we got to the partisans, I was weak with tuberculosis. They shaved my head because I had lice. They took away my crucifixes and told me I was Jewish. That was the lowest point in my life. I grabbed the scissors and didn't know who to kill—myself because I was bald, sick, and Jewish, or my mother because she was the cause of it all.

Once upon a time, a frightened but courageous Jewish mother placed her newborn baby boy with a non-Jewish family to save him from the wicked king's edict condemning all male newborns to death. Hopeful that the tyranny would end in her lifetime, she remained optimistic that her son would ultimately be reunited with his people.

And so he was. He grew up free of self-hatred, free of the humiliation of subjugation. He grew up with the self-esteem of a prince, having been raised as a royal son by a loving foster mother in the Egyptian Pharaoh's house. According to the Bible, Moses' birth mother was his wet-nurse, and as such stayed with him during his formative years. What the Bible does not tell us is at what age Moses discovered he was a Hebrew. But when the time came to rejoin his nation, he did so as their leader. His allegiance as an adult lay entirely with his biological people, and he identified with them wholeheartedly.

Three thousand years later, another despot came to power. He, too, had a Final Solution for the "Jewish problem." More than one million children perished as part of his plan, but a few hundred were saved by the non-Jews who raised them. Many were so young when they were placed in foster homes that later, when they were reclaimed by their parents, they did not remember them. These children were traumatized twice: first when they were removed from their parents, and again when they were reunited. Even if they were preverbal, the wrenching removal was still baffling and profoundly horrific. Not only were they transferred from home to home, but when they rejoined their Jewish parents, they had to leave the Church, which some of them had learned to love. Any sense of security or belonging or permanence was imperiled.

One form of damage to children who have been separated from their primary caretaker and/or subjected to multiple placements in successive homes, with foster parents or in institutions, is known as attachment disorder. Children with attachment disorder have difficulty trusting others. Some lose the ability to form loving relationships. After all, they have not had a consistent model of a lasting bond. They need to create self-protective barriers in order to avoid experiencing again the devastating loss of a loved one.

Not all children subjected to early separation suffer attachment disorder. Some, like Moses, receive so much affectionate nurturing in their infancy and early childhood that they develop the resources to withstand the trauma of change. Michael Lewis of the Institute for the Study of Child Development has been quoted as saying that events subsequent to the first year of life can be just as critical to psychological development. Children can learn not only to adapt, but to take initiative. They assume leadership roles and develop interpersonal skills, which they apply to their personal and later to their professional lives.

Among my interviewees, I found both types: people who were psychologically injured by their experiences, and people who emerged from their traumatic backgrounds with enhanced strengths and talents.

If anyone can be called a modern-day Moses, it is Abraham Foxman, national director of the Anti-Defamation League. Whenever there is a hiccup in the world Jewish community—a bias incident, a political development in Israel, a diplomatic brouhaha—the media turn to Abe Foxman for the Jewish reaction. But he is not just a spokesman who delivers pronouncements. He is a proactive leader who translates his vision of justice into policy and programs.

I met the fifty-eight-year-old, robust-looking Foxman in his Manhattan office in June 1998. When I walked in, he was in shirtsleeves, packing an already bulging briefcase with "homework." On his desk was a two-inch stack of messages. As I sat down, he shook my hand, quickly reread my letter of introduction, and started talking. He seemed very much in control of his remarks, but not rehearsed or stilted. On the contrary, he was warm and gracious. He talked about issues, rather than simply recounting his experiences. (His parents hid the infant Abe with his Catholic nanny, and when they came back for him five years later, she sued for custody and temporarily kidnapped him when she lost.) It was as though he were constantly taking care of business, the business of combating discrimination. His remarks were positive and thoughtful.

My Jewishness I had no choice about. Had my parents not survived I would have stayed Christian. I was five when they came back for me. There was a fierce custody trial, and if I'd been older, my caretaker would have won because they would have asked me to choose. I'm Jewish today because my parents made that decision. I think people have a tendency toward faith. People tend to be more believing. That doesn't mean they hold on to it all their lives. I was raised believing. I wore a crucifix. I went to church regularly. I cried when they called me Jew.

Now my father, the first time he took me to synagogue was on the holiday of Simchas Torah. He figured I'd like it because it's a joyous festival full of singing and dancing. (You can imagine that Simchas Torah in Vilna 1945, a city of one hundred thousand Jews that had three thousand left after the Liberation, was only relatively happy.) On the way there, I passed a church. I crossed myself, I greeted the priest, I kissed his hand, and my father understood. The Jewish children picked me up and danced with me, and I came home and told my mother, "I like Jewish church."

Little by little, he took off my cross and replaced it with arba konfos [a fringed ritual undergarment]. As long as I had substitution, I was happy. I used to say my prayers in Latin; he taught me to pray in Hebrew. Both languages were Greek to me. I was happy. I had substitution. He just said, don't kneel. Fine, it didn't matter. For a while, I went to church and synagogue. I prayed to God. It didn't matter which God. After the trial, I got into a Displaced Persons camp that was filled with Jews, a totally new environment for me. Becoming Jewish was a growing process.

My parents had wisdom beyond the normal. I asked my father once, why was my nanny so hateful at the end? After all, she loved me so much that she tried to kidnap me back from them. She had no other children, no husband. She had tried to get rid of my father under the Soviets. We sent her packages after the war. She signed for them, but never acknowledged them to us. He said, anything in excess is no good: too smart, too rich, too beautiful. She had too much love, and too much love gets perverted into hate.

I have photographs of her. When we crossed the borders, we went as displaced Turks. You had to discard any identifying belongings. I was told to play deaf and dumb because of the language. Later I realized that my father had smuggled out pictures of me and her. When I understood that that could have destroyed us, I asked him why he took the risk, and he said, "I was never sure if you would remember her without photos, and I wanted you to remember her. Not only did she risk her life to save you, but she saved us. We would have been much more vulnerable as a couple with an infant. A couple with a child can't move quickly, can't make decisions, can't take risks."

If my parents had perished, I would have been raised to be a priest. My caretaker believed in the Church. I was a good Catholic. In a courtyard after the war, my parents identified several children they knew to be Jewish orphans. In some cases they were successful at repatriation, sometimes not. Some of the families resisted because they loved the children or because they got money for keeping them. Ever since Madeleine, many more have come to the surface.

I'm convinced there are thousands of Jews who don't know they are Jewish, especially in Poland. Poland was the worst. There were more children at risk and therefore there were more opportunities to save them. Every day we lose potential Jewish souls there because their foster parents die without telling them they had Jewish parents. Either because they don't want to discombobulate their lives or because of the stigma of having saved Jews or because they feel guilty for not having told before. All these things conspire against truth-telling. Our agency tries to celebrate the idea of rescue in Poland. We try to make rescuing lives a value. We go there and applaud what they did so that it will be easier for the truth to come out. If the shame of helping Jews is removed, more revelations can surface. I've visited Poland three times, each time for a public effort to recognize Christian rescuers, and each time more Jewish children emerge.

The other thing we try to change is to get the Vatican to make available baptismal certificates so that those who suspect they are Jewish can go to the Vatican and find out. I was baptized, but my records have vanished. Either the Communists destroyed them or they were moved to the Vatican.

Circumcision also played a big role in survival. At the Hidden Children Conference, I looked out at the audience and noticed it was 90 percent women. That struck me for the first time. It was too dangerous to save boys. Some of the men were raised as girls. I was circumcised and therefore I couldn't play with anybody. It was too risky. My foster mother watched me like a hawk.

I asked Foxman how it happened that he devoted his life to Jewish community leadership as opposed to throwing up his hands and giving up on humanity.

I don't know. No idea. Anybody who tells you they know why they are in it is making up a story. My father must have had a lot to do with it. He was always active in Jewish life. He was a public figure before the war, during the war a bit, and after. Activism was in the house. He spoke, he wrote, he organized.

"You were never bitter?" I asked.

Who knows. I once consulted another survivor, a prominent therapist. Should I get therapy, I asked her. What for, she said, so you'll find out you resented your father? I'll tell you right now: there were two women who loved you and in order to reunite you with your father, you had to be separated from one of them so, yes, you resent your father. There. Now you know. Next?

So, who knows. It's nice to fantasize about why I do what I do. I deal with two elements of my formative years: I fight hate and I try to build bridges of understanding—which is what kept me alive. It sounds good, but I don't know how much is coincidence and how much is because of my background. I'm doing what I want to do. In my youth I wanted to be an engineer because Israel needed engineers and I wanted to move there. But I didn't like engineering and Israel didn't really need engineers, so I went to law school instead. Meanwhile I got married to someone who wanted to make her life in the States. In law school I decided I didn't want to practice law; I saw people who don't like what they do even though they make a lot of money. Sometimes kids rebel, sometimes they mimic their parents.

The Holocaust was always a subject in our house. My parents dealt with it. A lot of people didn't. My parents used to say, "Look at this—we lived it, and we still read all the books and see all the movies. And people who never lived through it say they can't bear to read about it or see the movies!"

I asked whether he knew Madeleine Albright.

We're friends. I understand her better than most, I think. Even if she knew, she didn't want to know. How could she? Her father converted when she was two. Think of it this way: Let's say I was raised as a Catholic, as she was. Let's say my parents perished and I'd become a priest, eventually a cardinal. Now my cousins from Tel Aviv write me a letter saying, you can't be a cardinal; you're Jewish. What would I do? I'd probably throw the letter in the garbage. If not, you put the lie to everything you have lived in the last fifty-some years, to everything your parents told you. And don't forget, hundreds of thousands died in Auschwitz who weren't Jewish, so dying in Auschwitz was no proof her grandparents were Jewish.

I joke that I'd like to put up signs that say, "Don't be anti-Semitic; after all, you, too, might turn out to be a Jew!"

The one thing hidden children had within their control was their silence. Their silence is what saved them. To this day, there are parents who will not discuss their experiences with their children. Then they go to a hidden child conference or they hear a talk by a survivor, and they open up.

Abe Foxman was only five when his parents came for him, but he was old enough to have formed an intense bond with his caretaker and her religion. It took time for him to transfer his loyalties, but with the help of supportive, patient, understanding parents, he succeeded in reclaiming his identity.

Many of the insights social psychologist and psychotherapist Eva Fogelman articulated with so much compassion in her essay, "Religious Transformation and Continuity," apply to those who told me their stories.

> When, in a desperate attempt to save their child from an imminent death, Jewish parents had the fortune to find a Christian family, or a convent, monastery, boarding school, or orphanage in which to hide their little one, placing the child was achieved with the utmost of love. Nevertheless, to the boy or girl, being placed felt like an abandonment and, indeed, often feels that way for the rest of his or her life.[1]

William Trost, a sixty-one-year-old antiques dealer born in Prague, was reunited with his parents at age four, but they had already rejected their Jewishness and put it behind them without ever telling young William about his heritage.

Many of the hidden children I interviewed had been through several successive intimate relationships, a history not uncommon among individuals who have suffered from attachment disorder to some degree. William has been married three times. To his knowledge, he is the youngest World War II refugee to travel to the United States alone. William's father came to America first, in 1940; his mother followed six months later. Before they left Europe, his parents placed him in a kindergarten in Zurich. They arranged for the woman who ran the child care facility to take the four-year-old out through France and Spain to Portugal, and to put him on a freighter. It was a perilous endeavor, but she succeeded. In January 1941, she placed young William onto a boat full of refugees headed for New York, and asked a sixteen-year-old girl to keep an eye on him.

I remember throwing up and waking up in vomit. I remember seeing the Statue of Liberty. And I remember the harbor being full of photographers when we landed.

First we lived in Elmhurst, Queens. My parents spoke German. I still understand it. When they wanted to talk secretly, they spoke Czech. Eventually we moved to Manhattan, where my father, who had been a banker in Europe, started acting strangely. It turned out he had syphilis, which had gone unchecked a long time. He took menial jobs while he could still work, and eventually died. My mother started out working in a greeting card factory, then a watch factory. Later she became secretary to a stockbroker, and when he passed away, she took over his work. She retired twenty years ago and moved to Germany with her Texan husband, a good-looking failed diplomat. She has supported them during their entire marriage.

For first grade I went to public school, but from second grade on they sent me to Catholic school. There was no religion at home, though. When I asked my mother, she said she was Lutheran. When my father's behavior deteriorated, they sent me to Catholic boarding schools. I hated it. I was miserable. I was also somewhat anti-Semitic as a result of what I was learning in school. In second grade, I remember there was a boy who invited me over to dinner. When he walked me home, he asked what temple I go to.

"I don't go to a temple. I'm Catholic."

"No, you're not. You're Jewish."

"No, I'm not!"

As soon as I got home, I told my mother how insulted I'd been. "He thinks I'm a Jew. Who the hell would want to be a Jew?"

I liked Catholicism until I was twelve or thirteen. Then things began to happen. I had a teacher who was not a Catholic brother. He let us talk freely about issues. I told him I was reading Voltaire in translation. The brothers were shocked and made me stop. By the time I left grammar school at age fourteen, I was disenchanted with Catholicism. My mother sent me to an all-boys high school. I ran away and only came back when she promised to send me to a nonreligious school.

My father's mother lived with us until the war ended. Then she went back to Czechoslovakia. My mother's parents hid with my cousin in Nice, France. When the Germans invaded, they hanged a few people and started looking for Jews. As long as my grandparents stayed indoors, they were safe, but one day in 1944, my grandfather said, "I have to get outside. It's a beautiful day. Nobody ever comes around here. I'm going to the tobacco store for cigarettes." Well, they got him. My grandmother turned herself in, in order to be with him.

I enrolled in the University of Pennsylvania as an English major. They had a junior year abroad program, and I decided on England. The day before my ship left, my mother told me to meet her after work at the cafeteria on Fifty-seventh and Lexington, across from the residential hotel we lived in at the time. "You're going to London. Your cousins from Surrey will meet you at the dock. They'll look after you." That's nice, I thought. She told me their names. "One other thing. They're Jewish." Okay, I thought. That's interesting. "You must understand. Since they're Jewish and they're related, you're Jewish, too!" "Okay." I didn't think much about it.

The next morning, I got into a cab with my mother and my stepfather. That's when I had the first massive anxiety attack of my life. It started a period of gruesome agoraphobia for twenty years, which only lessened when I began to face my anger about my withheld identity. Even though I was a lapsed Catholic, I was imbued with Catholic values, including anti-Semitism, so to find out I was Jewish was traumatic. It meant I was going to Hell. I knew I was in big trouble. With all the anxiety about my identity, agoraphobia was a natural reaction.

My English cousins told me that my mother's parents and lots of relatives had been killed in the Nazi death camps. I started having nightmares about the camps, guilt feelings about having been spared. And I was angry. Not only did my mother hide her *identity from me, but she also hid mine. And my father was her unwitting accomplice. That was so sick!*

William went back to Pennsylvania for his senior year, after which he got an exchange fellowship to the University of Bordeaux as a Fulbright scholar. He married the first woman he ever dated, a non-practicing French Catholic. They had a daughter, now in her mid-thirties. They did not give her any religious education, and today she is searching for her own spiritual path. When William and his first wife divorced, his wife moved to Washington, and their daughter decided to stay with William. She was eleven, and wanted to stay in her school, with her friends.

William's second marriage was to a Jewish woman. Her son and daughter had been raised Jewish, and William joined in her Jewish practices. "It was my first time in a community," he told me. "I liked it very much. It allowed me to get in touch with what it meant to be Jewish for the first time in my life."

Five years ago, William married a widow seventeen years his junior who had been brought up Catholic. Her first husband had been Jewish. "She's more Jewish than I am. We have Seders. We have lots of Jewish friends. She talks about converting. When she stops working she'll have time to study for conversion." William and his wife are not affiliated with a temple yet, but they intend to join one day. William works as a volunteer at the Jewish community center, giving English lessons to Soviet immigrants.

To this day, my mother pretends she's not Jewish. The England cousins were not practicing Jews, but at least they acknowledged who they were. My mother's explanation was, "We were labeled Jews but we were very assimilated. Anyway, who wants to be a Jew when you're so persecuted? I was protecting you."

There was something about the tightness in his voice as he uttered those last sentences that prompted me to ask William if he believed that she hid her Jewish identity in order to protect him. "No. She was just taking evasive action."

That last statement ran counter to the remarks, if not the conviction, of almost everyone else I interviewed. The others insisted that their parents must have withheld knowledge of their Jewish identity in order to make life easier, or even possible, for their children. The children may have been angry for a while on first learning of the deception, but eventually they squelched their resentment and transformed it instead into understanding and endorsement.

There was, however, another hidden child I interviewed who did not easily absolve parents of the responsibility to maintain and transmit their genuine identity. He was adamant that it is not healthy to back away from confronting the truth. Like others who have been raised under false pretenses, he has an impassioned commitment to honesty. And, although his story has striking parallels to that of William Trost, his reaction parallels that of Abe Foxman. Determined not to succumb to a pessimistic view of humanity, he has dedicated his professional life to combating racism and to celebrating acts of heroism and compassion.

I met Pierre Sauvage in a Manhattan cafeteria. As he strode purposefully down the aisle toward my booth, I recognized the filmmaker from his award-winning documentary, *Weapons of the Spirit*, a profile of the French town, Le Chambon-sur-Lignon, which hid five thousand Jews from the Nazis. Pierre's parents were among those five thousand, and Pierre was born during the Occupation, making him one of the youngest hidden children.

Concentrating on the righteous Gentiles who risked their lives to save others is a powerfully constructive way to salvage meaning from that black period of history. Pierre, who created the Chambon Foundation, has made a career of bringing to light positive models of human behavior.

Pierre was born in Le Chambon in March 1944. His parents raised him in hiding. What food there was, the farmers shared with their hidden charges—no complaints, no betrayals. The citizens of Le Chambon were the descendants of French Huguenots who themselves had experienced violent intolerance firsthand. Coming from a tradition of religious persecution and resistance, the villagers made helping others a critical element of their ethos.

After the war, Pierre's French father and Polish mother returned to Paris before moving to New York's Upper West Side when Pierre was four. He has no memory of the move, no recollection of learning a new language. The Upper West Side was and remains heavily Jewish. The Sauvages hid their Jewishness, although there was no need. They had been antireligious before the war, and remained so.

I wasn't raised Christian. I was raised as a "nothing." But we always had a tree on Christmas. My father did that well. Nothing in my adult years ever matched the excitement of going to bed and knowing presents would be there in the morning. My wife and I have done Chanukah with our kids, but it's not the same.

They sent me to a French private school, the Lycée Français de New York. They wanted me to be French, but on a subconscious level perhaps they also didn't want me to assimilate. The end result was that once I decided to reclaim my Jewish identity, it wasn't so difficult, because I was already different from the mainstream.

The number of children of Jewish refugees at my school was startling.

Of my four closest friends growing up, three were the children of refugees from Hitler's Europe. I had a comfort level with them. I guess my experience shaped me such that I gravitated toward people like myself. Most of my parents' friends were Jewish, too. My parents knew Yiddish but I never heard them speak it. It probably affected their way of thinking. I made a documentary on Yiddish, which won an Emmy. Even though I don't speak a word of Yiddish, I pulled the documentary together very fast. How the hell was I able to do that? I have to believe things are passed on even without labels.

I reconnected with some of my parents' friends later and asked if they knew my parents were Jewish. Some said, of course; others said, we suspected it of your mother. We had relatives nearby, but I never knew it. Everybody kept the secret. The amount of collusion was amazing.

Like William Trost, Pierre went abroad to continue his education. At age eighteen, on the eve of his departure for Paris, where he would live with his cousin, a survivor of Auschwitz, his parents sat him down and told him he was Jewish. Or that they were Jewish. Or that they had been born Jewish. He doesn't remember how they couched it.

Was it a shock? I don't remember. A surprise, for sure. They told me in such a way as to say, it's not important, and I accepted that characterization. Many years after my parents told me, I remained in hiding, in effect. I couldn't identify with it. It didn't feel like me. All those ten years in Paris, I never entered a synagogue. I had not one Jewish experience.

When a taboo is ostensibly *punctured, it isn't* necessarily *punctured. Its power lingers. You can tell a person a fact, but they don't really accept it fully. To this day I have difficulty remembering the names of my mother's dead relatives. I wasn't supposed to know, and I have to fight to feel entitled. The other result of being raised with secrets and taboos is that I am particularly sensitive to them. I'll reveal my deepest secrets to an audience of ten thousand. And people are responsive. I'll admit that I am rather proud that when I spoke to the American Psychiatric Association some years back, I got a standing ovation.*

As I made Weapons of the Spirit, *I got to know the people of Le Chambon who had saved my parents and so many others. It was these Christians who changed my views of religious people. The more I came to know and admire them, the more I came to realize that it was their strength of identity that made them act. They knew who they were.*

Weapons of the Spirit took seven years to make, and Pierre's son was born during that period. Having his first child and making that particular documentary were milestone events for him, and he became more Jewish in the process. He had married a "nice Jewish girl," and she insisted all along that a person's background matters.

Sauvage is friends with Helen Epstein, author of *Where She Came From: A Daughter's Search for Her Mother's Identity*, a biography of her Holocaust survivor mother as well as her grandmother and great-grandmother. In that work, she quotes Simone Weil, but she could just as easily have been quoting Pierre Sauvage. "To be rooted is perhaps the most important and least recognized need of the human soul. To be able to give, one has to possess; and we possess no other life, no other living sap, than the treasures stored up from the past and digested, assimilated and created afresh by us."[2]

In 1988, a scant week after his father died, Sauvage moderated and delivered introductory remarks at a panel discussion on "Shadows of the Holocaust: Reflections by the American and European Postwar Generation." Impelled by his commitment to honesty, he admitted to the audience that his film, *Weapons of the Spirit*, was the work not of a dutiful son but of a rebellious child. However, his reasoning for embracing Judaism in the face of his father's denial of it came from pure motives.

I am, perhaps, becoming a Jew, with the essential help of my wife and my eight-year-old son, and what I increasingly believe to be common sense: that one derives strength from being one's self, and that one's self is rooted, among other things, in one's heritage and one's history. When you erase your heritage, you rob your children of self-knowledge. Heritage is self-knowledge. That's an argument for religion, isn't it? The beliefs of your ancestors are part of you. They shaped you. To not know what shaped you is to be weakened.

Jews in Europe were at a disadvantage because their ancestry was easily traceable. The world, specifically the Nazi world at that time, did not extend to them the luxury of a chosen identity. Regardless of belief or practice, they were Jews by descent, and to be Jewish by descent, even partially, was to be condemned to death. Thus, converts to Christianity and intermarried assimilationists who did not consider themselves Jewish in the slightest were consigned to annihilation. Such a one was Portia Morgan's grandfather.

Portia's European-born mother suffers from generalized anxiety. She does not leave the house and will not speak of her past, but Portia knows something of her mother's history and was willing to share her knowledge. She has an uncle in Italy from whom she hopes to learn more family history as soon as she is able to visit. She told me that her mother, orphaned and then hidden in a convent, suffered multiple losses in adolescence, a crucial developmental age.

My mother's father grew up Jewish in Russia. He left for Italy right after the Revolution, and converted to Catholicism in order to marry my mother's mother. They raised their daughter (my mother) Catholic in the countryside. My mother's mother died of appendicitis when Mother was eleven. That was in the late thirties, when there was a lot of pressure to round up Jews. Her father was warned that even though he had converted long before, he was being considered Jewish and was on the list to be deported. His Catholic mother-in-law came from Rome to try to persuade him to hide or at least to give her the children, but he was adamant. He insisted that he was Catholic, more Catholic than the Pope, and in fact he was, but in the end it didn't matter. They took him to Auschwitz, where he was killed, vehemently denying all the time that he was Jewish. My mother got a postcard from him before he arrived in Auschwitz that said, "I'm fine. I'm well fed." She claims now that she thought he meant he was in summer camp.

Mother's Catholic grandmother was a wonderful person; her husband was not. That grandmother had to place her in a convent. One time some men came looking for Mother in the convent, and the nuns took her up to the attic to hide. The attic was full of people she hadn't known were there.

My mother is in denial about all that. Sometimes she laughs it off, saying she didn't know what was going on, even though for years all she had to eat was potatoes. She says she wasn't scared until much later, when she walked around Rome and saw the bodies of people who had been killed as punishment for hiding Jews.

My father is a WASP. He told me about my mother's childhood when I was pretty young because she started freaking out and he wanted me to understand why. She'd rather think it's a chemical disorder than work it through psychologically. We had a big fight when Madeleine Albright found out she was Jewish. I said, of all people, you should know how possible it is not to know you're Jewish. She just yelled at me. She didn't want to hear about it. "It's ridiculous," she said. "She's covering it up because she's ashamed, and that's terrible."

The truth is, her father died because he was born Jewish, and my mother suffered for that. She's not overtly anti-Semitic, but she criticizes Israel for its treatment of the Palestinians and she picks fights with the rabbi next door. One year the rabbi was celebrating a Jewish holiday with his family in their backyard, and she screamed at them for being too noisy.

Portia was raised nominally Christian. She is younger than her siblings by more than a decade. They were forced to go to church, but for her it was optional, "like dancing school." When Portia was at Barnard, which has a sizable Jewish population, she toyed with the idea of converting, but it was too overwhelming. She admires the Jewish emphasis on family and enjoys Jewish culture. Friends discouraged her from attending second generation meetings because she is not Jewish and she is younger than the average participant. They suggested that she would feel out of place.

My mother may suffer from survivor's guilt. After all, other people were killed or suffered in the camps. She may feel that her experience doesn't compare. She suffered but she doesn't admit the extent of it.

The cover story of the May 24, 1998, issue of the *New York Times Magazine*, "The Disconnected," is about children from Eastern European orphanages adopted by Americans. It describes the effects of parental deprivation and separations of parent and child. The article presents several informed but contradictory assertions about early separation: that it is harmful; that it is not necessarily harmful; that separation in and of itself is not the sole cause of personality disorders.

The article quotes psychoanalyst D. W. Winnicott as saying that an infant cannot develop an integrated personality absent a caretaker focused on his well-being. That statement could be applied equally to an uninterested too-young mother or to a foster parent who raises children for a fee, as a number of foster parents did during the Holocaust.

John Bowlby studied children who had been evacuated from London during the World War II blitz. He recorded a stage of grief or depression in the children, followed by an enduring emotional detachment. But in contrast to this blanket finding, developmental psychologist Mary Ainsworth intuited (according to "The Disconnected") that children who were securely attached at one year of age were those whose mothers responded quickly and astutely to their babies' cries in their first three months. And vice versa. Mothers who were distant or gruff had babies who were avoidant.

Indeed, some hidden children had loving caregivers and others were treated as unpaid servants. One cannot say all hidden children who had nurturing environments grew up secure, and all who endured a cold emotional atmosphere turned out sociopathic. But it makes sense that a child who receives warm parenting, whether from a biological parent or not, will have more emotional reserves to draw upon.

Harvard University child psychologist Jerome Kagan forestalls any generalization by arguing that each case must be judged individually. He credits inborn temperament with holding as much sway as circumstance in affecting personality. Psychological well-being depends to some extent on the child. Some are impervious to change, others are more easily traumatized.

This view is consistent with the range of stories I heard in the interviews. The most extreme reaction, of course, is suicide. One woman, a convert to Judaism of possible, if not probable, crypto-Jewish lineage, told me the story of her Italian-born husband, who had taken his own life. He had been given away as an infant because the people hiding his parents were afraid the baby's cries would betray their whereabouts. His parents placed him with a non-Jewish farm couple and returned for him after the war. The farmer was loath to give him back, so his mother persuaded the farmer to allow her to take the child out for a walk "to say goodbye." That was how she retrieved him.

He grew up, got married, and divulged what he knew of his history to his wife only when they were literally behind closed doors. Eventually he suffered a mental breakdown. Someone sent his widow an article contending that hidden children equate hiddenness with safety. Perhaps this grown hidden child's success made him feel exposed and endangered. But since he confided in no one, nobody will know what led to his final actions.

What is clear, though, is that his Jewish identity was restored when his mother recovered him. Of his own volition, he raised a Jewish family. The hidden children in contemporary Eastern Europe, who are now receiving attention from the media, from Jewish communal organizations, and from the psychological community, are learning as adults that they are of Jewish descent. Often, in fact, they simultaneously find out that the people they thought were their parents are not. As the World War II generation ages, they are making deathbed confessions to Jewish children whom they saved and raised as their own. Most of the Jewish parents met their death and never came back for them. The resurgence of Judaism in Poland, for example, has a large constituency from among those young adults who are finding out they are of Jewish descent.

Vera Frank did not initiate contact with me. I called her at the suggestion of a mutual acquaintance. She was not an eager interviewee, but not unwilling. She spoke in a slight, feminine, Polish-accented voice, utterly uninflected. Perhaps that is her defense—to put unbearable events at the wrong end of the telescope so that they are tiny and distant.

My parents came from the same province in Poland. They married when they were in their twenties. I had a sister ten years older and a twin brother. We lived in the ghetto without my father, who was a prisoner of war in Russia. He left when I was three and a half months old. It was hard on everybody there, not just Jews. Everyone was starving and freezing.

The worst time was when I was three and a half years old. By then I had forgotten my father completely. The Nazis came to where we were staying for a "selection." This time they were selecting [for death] anybody who could not work as a slave laborer, meaning old people and children. When my mother saw that they were going to take me and my brother and sister away, she ran upstairs and jumped out the window. My brother doesn't remember, but I will never forget. I saw her body. He didn't.

The Nazis knew that if they took us away in this situation, there would be a riot in the ghetto, so they left us alone for the time being. My aunt who was with us gave me to a Christian friend outside the ghetto. They were religious Catholics. They gave me a Polish name and told people I was their illegitimate child. They said I was younger than I was, which was easy to believe because I was so undernourished. I stayed with them for four years. It was very brave of them to take me in. They were really righteous Gentiles. They were very good to me. The woman was pregnant with her own daughter when they took me. I fell in love with them and they with me. They said they would never give me back. They treated me as their own.

The husband was shot two months after they took me in, for working for the underground. He was an only child. His father, my Polish grandfather, became an alcoholic. He never loved me. He hated everybody. He abused everyone physically and mentally. My Polish mother was afraid of him. After the war, my Polish mother contacted the Jewish community about me and asked for some financial support. They gave her an apartment in exchange for her promise to send me to Hebrew class. But once I got involved in the Jewish community, they wanted to send me to Israel. I was put on a train, but I was a very smart child. I escaped and ran back to my Polish grandfather.

The whole four years I was with them, I had no contact with my aunt. I never saw her again. (When I went to Israel, I found out that she and her children had been killed in the Majdanek death camp.) Apparently, she had told everybody she met that she had hidden me with this family, so that after the war maybe some relative would come for me. Well, in 1945, when I was six, my father found me. He showed my photo to my Polish grandfather, who demanded money. My father paid him and that was that. My father put me in a cab and we moved right away to the city. My grandfather never told his daughter what happened, and she never got a penny of the payment.

I was terrified. What does this Jew want with me? I didn't understand his language. I didn't understand why he was kidnapping me. All I could think was that it was almost Passover and he needed a gentile child's blood to make matzo. That's what we had been taught.

In her psychological practice, Eva Fogelman has heard words like these more than once. With her training and insight, she hears the anxieties behind the words. As she puts it:

> The life-sized paintings of a mother protecting her child, the soothing music and liturgy, the incense, the sense of belonging, being told "Mary and Jesus love you and will protect you forever"—all of this began to alleviate some of the emotional pain and replaced the impotent Jewish God. The only drawback to this new protected state was that the child's life was threatened if he or she did not remain loyal to Mary and Jesus. Hell was the penalty for disloyalty.
>
> Continue the scenario: one year later—or, for some, five years later—a total stranger comes to take you out of the hiding place. This stranger could be your own father or mother, an aunt, or a representative of a Jewish organization. These new caretakers remove the cross from around your neck and throw out your Christian prayerbook. You begin to see images of Hell, and you know that you will end up there if you abandon Mary and Jesus.[3]

It was years until Vera was able to understand what was happening to her. Her father was kind, but his second wife was not. She was a survivor of Auschwitz and jealous of her stepdaughter. She never had children with Vera's father, and her own children from her previous marriage perished in the war.

Every year Vera's father applied to move from Poland to Israel. Finally, in 1957, they emigrated. She met her husband, also a survivor, in Israel, and they have a daughter, an only child.

I asked Vera if her daughter knew her history. "Of course. I told her about it right away. From the beginning. Listen, if I could take living it, she can take hearing it as a story."

I made the observation that many children of survivors found it helpful to go to support groups, and that survivors themselves had found such groups uplifting and enlightening. "I went to parenting groups much later. My daughter is named after my mother. She has three girls. They lead a traditional Jewish life. They live nearby. My husband needs the phone now, and, anyway, we are finished talking."

Before she could hang up, I requested an appointment to talk with her brother; surprisingly, she continued speaking. She explained that her brother spoke only Polish.

Three years ago my girlfriend sent me a clipping of an interview with a hidden child in Poland. She knew I had been hidden, and thought I would be interested. When I saw the photo, I realized that the man who gave the interview looked like my biological grandfather. Three months earlier I had gone to my aunt's funeral and found a picture of my grandfather. I wrote to the interviewer and got the name and phone number of the hidden child. I called him and we compared memories. I figured out that he was my twin brother, but I had to convince him. We had the same nickname, Ketzl, pussycat. And we compared birth dates. I sent him photos. I have one of my mother holding the two of us on her lap. His son looks exactly like our father.

He was very shocked. He didn't remember having a family. He didn't remember the suicide. His foster parents had taken him from the Majdanek orphanage. He thought they did it to save his life, but they took him for money. They raised him Catholic. They had six biological children after him. He was the oldest. He always felt like a third wheel. He felt he didn't belong. They used him as a babysitter, housecleaner, errand boy. He suspected he wasn't theirs because he was circumcised. At age six, the other kids threw him into the water, calling him Obrzezany, the Circumcised One. He asked his parents, but they told him he was illegitimate. They always told him a different story. He wanted to look for his parents, but he didn't even know their name.

When my brother's Polish Catholic wife found out he was definitely Jewish, it put a lot of pressure on their marriage and they divorced. He was never a devoted Catholic. For myself, I feel Jewish, but I'm not observant. So now he's here and she's there with their three boys and the grandchildren. The kids didn't want anyone to know they were part Jewish.

It was a struggle to get permission for him to stay here. We have no papers proving we're related. We fought with immigration and contacted our Congressman. We collected signatures. Finally he was granted residency as a humanitarian gesture.

It was a relief when he was found, because he always suspected he was Jewish. The news filled the empty space in my soul and in his.

Whereas Vera spoke in a dispassionate voice, Stefa Hasson literally overflowed with feeling. Her face flushed with emotion as she narrated her poignant history, and we had to stop several times for her to collect herself. A teacher in a Jewish day school, Stefa gives tours in her off hours at the Museum of Jewish Heritage, which is how I found her.

My mother was the youngest of nine children. She might have been a change of life child. There were ten years between my mother and her older sister. She was on her own at a very young age.

I was born during the war in the Lvov ghetto. It was dangerous to have an infant during the round-ups because you couldn't hide a crying baby. They must have given me sleeping pills. There were more and more round-ups. The Lvov ghetto was being liquidated. One day my father just never came back. He'd been killed. I was an infant, their only child. When my mother decided to jump the ghetto wall, she tried to persuade her nine-year-old nephew to jump, too, but he wouldn't leave his mother. "She won't know where I am. She'll be worried."

My mother thought, "alles eince" [it's all the same]: we're going to die here anyway, so we might as well try something. It's only a matter of time. The nephew threw me over. I was only an infant. It was a bitter cold night. Mother was afraid we would freeze. My father had a chocolate shop before the war. She said my father was a "draw," that because he was good-looking, people came into the store. He probably was handsome, but my mother thought everyone was good-looking. That's really how she saw people. Anyway, that night she knocked on the door of a former customer. Maybe they had a credit line at the store. In any event, it was awkward. There were Nazis in the house. They probably played with me that night! It was obvious we couldn't stay beyond the one night.

My mother found us a shack on the outskirts of Lvov, along the railroad tracks. She posed as the wife of a Polish soldier, waiting for her husband's return from the front. She bootlegged to support us. Every morning she would go out foraging for things to sell. She left me in the middle of the bed, with an apple to eat and a comb to play with and a dog named Mikuzck to watch me until she returned at night. Imagine—a dog was my babysitter. Nowadays we would NEVER *leave a toddler unattended with an apple, but . . . One day I slithered off the bed and started toddling toward the tracks. The dog wasn't able to stop me. Somebody noticed and picked me up. Those were the people who kept me.*

At this point, Stefa was overcome with emotion and apologized for crying. I was surprised because I had been under the impression that, as a docent at the museum, she told her story several times a day. I was wrong. This was uncharted territory. She had told some of it to family or Holocaust study groups, but it was not part of her docent's script.

The husband was a musician and lived with his wife and mother-in-law. I think they were Protestants. I don't really know. They didn't press us about our identity. It was dangerous for them to know. It must have been pretty obvious, but they never asked. They invited us to stay with them. They had no children of their own. My mother changed her last name to Levitska. It sounds Jewish to me, like Levy, so I'm not sure what she thought she was accomplishing. I had been born Sarah. That became Sabina, and finally, for safety's sake, I became known as Stefa, after a Polish saint.

It's funny how long it takes sometimes to understand things in retrospect. My son plays violin. (Of course he would choose the violin—after all, we own a piano!) He's very talented and joined a youth symphony, which meant that I had to carpool him back and forth several evenings a week, and wait for him during concerts and rehearsals. The funny thing is, I never minded waiting. I felt extremely comfortable at rehearsals. It's only in the last few months that I came to the realization that the reason I felt so comfortable is because my Polish father used to take me to rehearsals with him all the time. I would sit on the floor off to the side while the orchestra rehearsed. So when my son went to rehearsals, it was like coming home.

Those years were in a way a good time for me. I was the darling of my mother, of Mamcha (my Polish mother), of her mother, and of my Polish father. I became a Christian then. I remember the Christmas tree with candy hanging from the boughs.

One time, I was playing in the courtyard. There were apartments all around. There must have been an old Jewish woman hiding there, because the soldiers came and dragged her out. She was screaming, "I'm not Jewish! I'm Polish, skin and bones!" That must have been some kind of colloquial expression, but you know how kids mix things up. The next few days, we reenacted that scene in our play, yelling, "We're Christians, with half a pound of bones!"

At some point my mother left. I don't know why or how. I don't remember her leaving. But I vividly remember how it was when she came back and I had to leave my Polish mother. It was terrible. They must have walked me part-way down the road to meet my mother. I guess the war was over, and she was able to be reunited with me. We were going to Bergen-Belsen, which became a displaced persons camp. I was three or four years old. I didn't understand why I couldn't have two mothers. I was crying so hard.

The first time I saw Jews I was scared out of my mind. They were bearded Hasidim, dressed in black. They looked demonic to me. After a while, I became an ardent Zionist in the camp. I must have known all our family had been killed, and Israel seemed the only hope. I loved my Polish parents, but I had no positive feelings toward the Polish people as a whole. I'll never forget that first Yom Kippur in Bergen-Belsen. The Yizkor memorial prayer was not to be believed. But for over a year in the camp, I used to hide in a closet and kneel down to the Virgin Mary in prayer.

There were several men interested in my mother, but she wanted me to choose a husband for her because her priority was my happiness. I chose my father because he came that first time with thirty-six Hershey's chocolate almond bars. That did it for me. It was a good choice. Children loved him. He was a wonderful man and a wonderful grandfather to my kids. He himself had lost a wife and four children in concentration camp. As much as I liked him at the time, though, I had tremendous anxiety that maybe my father wasn't really dead and would come back, and I would have to choose between them.

We moved to the States in the fifties. There was a housing shortage, and we had to bribe our way into an apartment house. When the ownership changed hands, it became a slum. It was a strange childhood. I learned English, my parents didn't, so at age twelve I had to go to the housing authority with them and argue for our rights. We were supposed to go to Israel, and we packed a trunk. My mother had raised geese and plucked the feathers herself to make a comforter. We kept the comforter in the trunk. In the slum, the ceiling leaked and ruined the comforter, so there, in the small claims court, it was me and a rotten trunk of feathers. The landlord was an attorney by profession. We won. Can you imagine?

My mother was not going to be defeated. She was a collector of people. I suppose she was lonely for all the people she lost. She even became friends with her second husband's previous in-laws [his first wife's parents].

We stayed in touch with my Polish parents. We sent reeds for his clarinet, and food and clothing.[4] *My mother sent care packages to lots of Polish Christians she had been friends with before the war. She was a very caring person, always on the phone with this one or that one—so much so that sometimes I resented it, feeling neglected.*

She was a very Jewish person. We joined a synagogue. She said the rabbi reminded her of her father. She once bought a painting of a bearded Orthodox-looking man. She said it reminded her of her father. I enjoy Jewish things. My husband is Sephardic, from Salonika, Greece. My mother-in-law once showed me his baby pictures. In one of them, he's in a baby carriage. At that age, I was being kept in a dresser drawer.

I think of myself as a "bridge" person. I still wonder, which God saved me, the Jewish God or the Christian? Why could I not have been saved as a Jewish person? Why did I have to become Christian in order to survive? I heard a rabbi say that it's arrogant to think you can understand everything.

The things I planned never happened. I planned to go to Israel. I was devastated when we couldn't go there after the war. On the other hand, things I never planned did *happen. There seems to be a design to my life. I never intended to send my children to Jewish day school, but my friend did, so I followed. I never intended to teach social studies in a Jewish day school, but here I am. I never even applied for the job! I made a conscious decision to be Jewish, partly out of a sense of outrage—nobody has the right to go after my family just because we're Jewish. I won't give in to that. And partly out of a sense of obligation to my ancestors.*

I figure God must like variety because He made all kinds. I don't reject any one denomination. The Jewish people are small enough in number. We need to accept people, not reject them.

Stefa is ensconced in a traditional Jewish East Coast community. Ethnically and culturally, she lives a Jewish lifestyle, but on one level, probably religiously, she calls herself a bridge person. She was raised by loving Catholics and by a loving Jewish mother, so both religions have been "good to her."

Rene Lichtman declares himself an atheist but identifies strongly as a Jew. Though not quite as fortunate as Stefa, Rene also chose to align himself with the Jewish community and for the same reason—"I felt a responsibility to become a Jew because we were almost exterminated." Jews who have been targeted as such by outsiders often turn around and embrace their assigned identity. From identity-by-descent comes identity-by-consent.

Rene's life was a pinball game of ricocheting from home to home, country to country. Born in France, Rene was two and a half when the Germans invaded. His father had joined the French Army some months before, and asked a Christian family outside Paris to care for Rene should anything happen. The family ran a day care center for working parents, and agreed to take Rene in, probably, he thinks, because the wife was fond of his father. Rene's father was killed early in the fighting, and his mother went into hiding. His entire family, save an aunt and three cousins, perished. Rene thinks that his current activist political stance is a result of having a father who fought in the war, and that his Jewish identity consists of belonging to a people that is persecuted for no reason other than who they are.

When Rene was seven, his mother showed up at the day care center to take him with her. He passively accepted the news that this stranger was his mother and that he was Jewish.

She was very attractive. Sang beautifully, had a strong, cheerful personality. But our communication was nonexistent. She couldn't talk about my father to me. That was the tragedy of our relationship. Maybe she didn't understand what it is to have a child. Maybe she felt guilty because she hadn't raised me. She had a boyfriend in Paris, but it didn't work out, so in 1950, we went to the U.S. to meet an elderly Jewish widower my aunt wanted to introduce to her. He was already a grandfather when they got married.

He couldn't deal with me at all. I was out of control in response to the rejection I had suffered and of not knowing who I was. First I was French. Then I didn't want to be because the French were anti-Semitic.

So I became Americanized. I was twelve and a half, a pivotal age for language, and I lost my accent totally. Six months later, I'm bar mitzvahed and expected to learn Hebrew. And then there was the matter of names. I had three last names, and my first name changed from Rene to Ronald. By then I had an ulcer, which annoyed my stepfather.

He was a religious man, but not spiritual. Very strict, cold and mechanical. I realized that I was not a believing person. It didn't make sense to me. My guardians had talked to me about Jesus, but it never made an impact. It just doesn't make sense that God would let all that crap happen. By seventeen I decided to join the army to get away. I think I've always been an atheist. A cultural Jew, yes, with a strong identification with all the Jews who suffered in Europe. A lot of hidden children are ambivalent about who they are. They feel more comfortable in a church setting.

My wife's father is Jewish. Only when we had kids did I realize I wanted them to know about Judaism, especially the history, and especially Eastern European history. When they were little, we had a Christmas tree out of respect for my mother-in-law. I thought our kids should know that side of the family, their dual heritage, but after a few years we decided it was too confusing, so we became more traditionally Jewish. My wife converted and has been learning Hebrew. I think she has a stronger belief in a Jewish God than I do. Our kids have had a good Reform Jewish education. Two of them have been to Israel.

I stayed in touch with my foster parents for years. I went back in 1964, to say goodbye really. The husband had died, and the wife was ill and elderly. They had made plans for me to be an artist if nobody were to come for me. They thought of me as their son, and I felt it.

I'm very active with hidden children here. I went to the 1991 world conference. We had so much in common, it was unbelievable. There were people there who had never talked about their experiences before, not even to their children. There are a lot of people who say we have enough programs on the Holocaust. They say you can't build identity on negatives. I don't disagree with that, but we need both. You have to look to the future.

Eric Cahn was at that 1991 conference. He did not talk about his wartime experiences until the late 1980s—not even to his children.

Eric's family was deported to Camp Gurz in France in October 1940. His parents "made the difficult and heart-wrenching decision" to hide their children with the French Resistance. One month later, on September 16, his parents were put in a cattle car to Auschwitz. From Serge Klarsfeld's book on the death camp, Eric learned that his mother was killed on arrival.

The Resistance found homes for Eric and his sister. Eric was four and a half. He was kept in a basement.

I was there for a year and a half. It was confusing. I had no idea why I was there. I spent the time sleeping and crying. I looked forward to them coming down and talking to me. They had to be very careful. The Nazis occupied the town. The family convinced me to be quiet as much as possible. They took good care of me. They brought me food and, whenever they could, they took me outside. Usually at night. I remember how much I looked forward to fresh air. I had no relationship with other children, which had an effect on who I am today.

After the war, my French Christian family reunited me with my sister in a Jewish orphanage. Then our father tracked us down. We lived with him from 1946 to 1950, when he sent us to America. I never forgave him for that.

We lived in Colorado with our maternal grandparents, who had escaped from Europe with five children in 1939. They resented having us dumped on them. My sister thinks they especially disliked me because I look like my mother. When they retired, they shipped us off to an orphanage. That place gave me my first positive sense of being. The administrator turned out to be someone I could relate to. He took an interest in me as an individual. But once we finished high school, my sister and I were on our own.

I've been married twice, both times to non-Jews. I consider myself Jewish. I am circumcised and had a bar mitzvah. My two older children have grown up with the traditions, but they are not practicing anything.

I didn't talk about my childhood until my kids were teenagers, when I thought they could handle it, but I see I could have opened up earlier, because my twelve-year-old is having no problem. I guess I wasn't ready. Now I talk to student groups about hate and what it can lead to. World War II didn't end in 1945 for people like me.

Halina Singer could not talk about her wartime experiences as a hidden child until she went back to Poland in 1995. She says that traveling to the convent she lived in from age four to age eight was like closing a circle in her life. Until she literally and figuratively revisited the past, she could not put it to rest.

I had tea with Halina, now called by her Hebrew name, Chaya, in a suburb of Tel Aviv. The walls of her immaculate apartment are covered with artwork. Chaya herself is a vivacious redhead with sparkling eyes, but her cheerfulness is tempered by sadness and what felt to me like resignation, or perhaps acceptance. She was born in Warsaw in 1938 to a wealthy family, which owned a cosmetics shop in a predominantly Catholic neighborhood of Puavska.

The war broke out when she was two, and her father was deported and killed early on. Her mother gave Halina to one of the unmarried manicurists, Mariska, who worked for the family.

She told Mariska that if she never makes it out alive, Mariska could keep our house and all our possessions. She should just promise to raise me well. I lived with them for two years, but the upstairs neighbors called the Gestapo, suspecting I was a Jewish child.

The first time the Gestapo came, Mariska and her father, Sigmund, hid me under the sofa. The Gestapo pierced it with bayonets and almost found me but my parents bribed them to stop and leave. The neighbors called them again and told them to look harder. Sigmund had just enough warning to get me onto a meat truck. He woke me up in the middle of the night, told me to get dressed, and lifted me onto the truck, where I hid between two carcasses whose blood stained my clothes. We drove to a convent that took in orphans and he told the nuns that he found me wandering the streets, bloodied and obviously orphaned. He explained that he couldn't possibly take me in and would they please accept me. He was a very smart man, Sigmund. He once saw a girl also named Halina being buried, and he stole her papers. That's how he proved to the nuns that I was a Christian.

Life in the orphanage was hard, but we didn't realize it so much because we were all equally deprived. There was no food to speak of, just watery soup and chunks of potato or a slice of bread. The nuns were very strict. Our day was made up of prayer and study. We learned that the

Jews killed Jesus. There was a set of clothes and shoes in one size, so if you were the right size, that's what you wore. If not, you wrapped yourself in curtains and went barefoot, meaning you could not go outside. That's why I was indoors looking out the second-story window with my girlfriend when my mother showed up.

My mother had been sent to the Warsaw ghetto, but she escaped almost immediately. She went to work as a maid for a family called Ewing. They were so anti-Semitic that if they found a Jew, they would set their dogs on him. Of course they had no idea my mother was Jewish. After the war, we found out an extremely ironic incident. The mother superior of my convent was obsessed with the Snow White story, and every year she would have us put on a show. Mrs. Ewing went to the orphanage to donate some money and sat through one of the performances. She reported back to my mother that there was one particular dwarf who was unusually adorable. We figured out later that it was me she had been talking about.

After the war, when I was eight, my mother went to Mariska's house to look for me, but the house was mostly torn down. She didn't know if I was dead or alive, but she wouldn't stop looking for me until she knew for sure. She went from orphanage to orphanage. My friend and I were looking out the window. I remember we were laughing about something, when we saw a woman in a leopard-skin coat walk up the path. I said to my friend, my mother had such a coat. It was my mother. She kept the coat hoping I would recognize it. She had only rags on underneath.

She told the mother superior that she was looking for a place to volunteer her services. She examined each child, and when she got to me she stared for a long time and searched my neck for my birthmark. The mother superior asked me, "Do you know who this lady is?" and I automatically replied, "She's my mother." I don't know why I said it, and nobody paid attention.

My mother worked there as a volunteer, and made sure to stay close to me. She got me used to her. One day, she took me away with her to the partisans. The nuns didn't make much of a fuss because it meant one less mouth to feed. As we traveled, I would kneel and cross myself every time we passed a statue of Mary. My mother asked me if I love Jesus. "Of course." I told her Jesus was killed by the Jews. She said nothing.

When we got to the partisans, I was weak with tuberculosis. They shaved my head because I had lice. They took away my crucifixes and told me I was Jewish. That was the lowest point in my life. I grabbed the scissors and didn't know who to kill—myself because I was bald, sick, and Jewish, or my mother because she was the cause of it all.

We stayed with the partisans until the Jewish Agency took us to Israel. My mother met a starving Russian Jew who had lost his entire family. She brought him back to life by feeding him birdseed, which was all she could find. They married and he adopted me. He raised me as his own. I was so close to him, that it wasn't until after he died that I told my two sons that he had been my stepfather, not my father. As an adult, I finally asked my mother to tell me about my biological father, but she said it was too far in the past to talk about.

My mother stayed in touch with Mariska and Sigmund after the war. She sent them packages until the Six-Day War in 1967, when they told her the atmosphere in Poland was too anti-Israel. It became dangerous for them to receive anything from us. We started writing again in 1986, and in 1989 my mother visited them. Sigmund told her he had a hard time finding work in Poland because he was known to have sheltered a Jewish girl during the war.

After my mother died, I tried to keep up the correspondence, but even though I am fluent in spoken Polish, my mother tongue, I'm not so good at writing it. I wrote to them, but in my last line I said, if this letter is too hard to read, you can call me in Israel. Here is my phone number. Well, two weeks later, the phone rang. It was Mariska's son, Michael. He told me that Mariska had recently died, but he wanted us to stay in touch. He thought of me as a sister. He came for a two-week visit, and I don't think we ever went to sleep. We just talked and talked, day and night.

Then, it was my turn to visit Poland. He took me to his old house. The only part left standing was the room with the sofa I hid under during the Gestapo raid. I walked in and I could picture the piano, the desk. I was paralyzed, unable to move. He pointed to where the second floor would have been and told me that was the apartment of the neighbors who betrayed me. It was just as I remembered, and I burst out crying. It was a long time until I could stop crying.

Michael asked me what he could do for me. I said there were two things I wanted to accomplish on my visit. I would like to visit Ger, the city where my mother grew up, and I would like to see the convent. We went to Ger. There is one Jew left. He takes care of the cemetery, because he had promised his father he would. Still, it's in terrible condition. I looked for headstones that said either Polonetsky, my mother's family, or Richheiser, my father's. No luck.

Then we went to the convent. It was in a region full of sanatoriums for tuberculosis. Where the convent should have stood was a brand new building for the treatment of children born with a cleft palate. We found an older nun and told her what we were looking for. She told us that, yes, there used to be an old building around the side that served as an orphanage. She walked us around the building and I could make out the faint trail of a worn-out path. That was the path my mother walked up when I spotted her out the window. We left through the courtyard. In the middle stood a statue of one of the Seven Dwarfs!

This trip gave me closure. Until then I had never been able to talk about my experience. It was like an open wound. Now I was more at peace than I had ever been. It's funny. During my first few years in Israel, I used to beg my mother to take me to Haifa. I didn't know why, exactly, but I felt a pull to go there. When we went, I headed straight for the church that is featured in all the posters of Haifa. Apparently, I had a need to make that contact. Even as recently as five years ago, when I toured Haifa, I felt a magnetic pull to walk into a church. No more. Not since my visit to Poland.

When I was young, I knew I was Christian. Then I was told I was Jewish. In Israel, I couldn't stand it when people would pinch my cheeks and call me "Yiddishe boobah" [little Jewish doll]. I didn't know who I was or where I belonged. It took time, but eventually living in Israel gave me strength. After that visit to Poland in 1995, I made a clean break with the past. That's when I was able to end my silence and talk about my life.

A year and a half ago, I visited my son, who is studying for his post-doctorate in America. My daughter-in-law convinced me to record my story in the Washington, D.C., Holocaust museum. I did the same for Kibbutz Lochamei HaGetta'ot [Ghetto Fighters], which has a project devoted to Hidden Children.

I thought I had paid all the dues I would have to in this life, but in 1987, on a trip to Brazil with my husband, we were in a traffic accident.

He was killed and I suffered serious injuries. I came back to Israel ten days later, and my friends nursed me back to health. Holocaust survivors don't have large families, but our network of friends is just amazing.

I don't blame anyone for what happened to me. It was simply a period in history, and people got caught up in what was going on. I'm not an observant Jew, but I'm definitely a believer and I certainly think of myself as Jewish.

Eva Fogelman seems to equate the Jewish self with memories, tastes, smells—in other words, with a gestalt as opposed to a genetic inheritance. Yet, like Jerome Kagan, she suggests that the innate ability to cope with shifting circumstances helps an individual regain an integrated sense of wholeness, of identity.

There was an interplay of heritage and choice when a hidden child recovered his past. But what a complicated dilemma: One could choose the religion of one's biological parents—and if those parents returned, that choice became the more compelling. One could choose the religion of the foster home, be it an individual or an institution. Or one could renounce religion altogether, which, for a person who was persecuted for reasons of religion, might appear a logical, even attractive alternative.

To end with Fogelman's words:

> The "self" of hidden children underwent several transformations. The ability to withstand such fragmentation of the self and inner chaos was compounded by the fear of Purgatory. Hence, to adjust to such disequilibrium, one needed to achieve a mode of flexible psychological coping.
>
> For some hidden children, becoming Jewish after liberation was a continuity to their prior self; while for others it was a discontinuity. They had no memories, no tastes, no smells, no symbols as reminders of their Jewish self. In countries where it was difficult to live openly as a Jew, many hidden children knowingly or unknowingly continued to live as Catholics or Protestants. Without a community with which to share one's beliefs, particularly as a Jew, it is troubling and puzzling to be a Jew . . . The richness of the Jewish way of life with its own recurring annual events and life-cycle rituals is mean-

ingless if one only knows what it means to be a Jew from his or her own personal suffering during the years of the Hurban (Destruction). It is the connectedness to the destroyed pre-Holocaust life that ultimately will integrate the fragmented self of the hidden children, and thereby of future generations.[5]

Children of Survivors

Like many newly arrived families, we immersed ourselves in the business of making a living and fitting in. I always had the feeling that we had Jewish family or were Jewish ourselves, but I was not able to actually ask the question. When I did ask my mother about it during her last illness in 1979, her answer was, "No, we have no Jewish relatives." Then, when I started working on our genealogy, my father also denied having any Jewish relatives, but the way he answered always raised more questions.

Helen Epstein was born to two Holocaust survivors in 1947, two years after the end of the War. Thirty years later she began the research that would culminate in her book, *Children of the Holocaust: Conversations with Sons and Daughters of Survivors.*[1] She and her peers, fellow children of survivors, had reached an age when they could take a retrospective look at their lives and try to reach an understanding of how their upbringing differed from, shall we say, normal experiences.

Some of the recurring threads in Epstein's interviews included parents who, because they had lost their own parents so young, had no model from whom to learn how to bring up a child. Some interviewees mentioned distant parents who, having endured wrenching loss, were afraid to establish close emotional bonds for fear those bonds would be violently severed again. Others talked about parental episodes of profound depression, extended unexplained silences, or severe temper tantrums.

Children of survivors are exquisitely sensitive to their parents' history. They dare not add to their parents' abundant measure of anguish. Even into adulthood, these children are careful to shield their parents from bad news, from failure, from any more blows to the psyche. They instinctively know that if their parents have not been forthcoming with information, they are not to initiate a painful discussion, even if they come across indisputable evidence of the unmentionable past.

All these patterns surfaced in my interviews. The difference, though, between the people I interviewed and those whom Epstein interviewed, is that I was speaking exclusively to people who did not know their parents had suffered under the Nazi regime.

Yossi, a fair-haired, fair-skinned, middle-aged Dutchman of trim build, met me in a quiet Tel Aviv café, wearing a plaid shirt, chinos, and a skullcap. He was coming straight from the army's National Defense College in Tel Aviv, where he was spending his mornings for one year, before returning home in the afternoons to his wife and five children in Jerusalem. Because it is not his mother tongue, Yossi spoke a rather formal, book-learned English, but the more he relaxed, the more colloquial his language became.

My mother was born in Amsterdam in 1918 to an Orthodox family. She was one of five siblings. Her father was the hazzan *[cantor] of the synagogue. My mother, who was a nurse, and two of her brothers went to work in 1937 in a Jewish psychiatric facility. Three years later, the rest of the family, including my mother's fiancé, was rounded up in a Nazi raid. They were deported and killed, which my mother found out for certain only after the War.*

In 1942, the psychiatric hospital received advance word that the Nazis were coming for them. They released the ambulatory patients and much of the staff. Some of the staff, including my mother's two brothers, volunteered to stay with the bedridden patients. They were all deported and killed. My mother, meanwhile, was hidden along with three or four others in the basement of a mansion by an unmarried Christian woman in a wealthy neighborhood. For three years she did not see the light of day. Even now, when we go camping, for example, she quakes at any unexplained noise and can't relax until she knows what it is, for fear of Nazi footsteps.

When the war ended, my mother was determined that no family of hers would ever be targeted by Nazis again, so she cut all her ties with the past. Having come from a practicing family, this was a traumatic break with Judaism, but she had lost her faith and suffered tremendous anxiety about anti-Semitism. She returned to nursing, and seven years later married my non-Jewish father, whom she met at a table tennis match. He found her white nurse's uniform distracting as he played, and went over to ask her to sit further away from the tournament table.

When he proposed, she told him she was Jewish, but swore him to secrecy. She believes there should be no lies between husband and wife. My father is from a Socialist/humanist background. His family was very committed to human rights, and had a live-and-let-live attitude. My father's study of the history of human civilization convinced him that organized religion had done more harm than good over the centuries, but he was in no way against religious people. He himself had no religious affiliation. Growing up we had a Christmas tree, but it had no religious significance for us. We did not even have a Bible in the house, and I was probably the only child in my public school who never heard of Abraham or Moses or the Exodus from Egypt.

One day when I was fourteen, the newspaper was thrown through the mail slot in the door, and I heard my mother wail, "Oh no, not again." It was many years before I figured out what "again" referred to. I instinctively turned to the paper she was staring at and read the headline, which was in much larger print than usual: "ISRAEL AT WAR AGAIN." *I had never heard of Israel, but I read the paper, which had lots of background articles about modern Israeli history from 1948 to the present. I found it fascinating, so I went to the library and took out some books about Israel. It became a hobby for me, like stamp collecting. The history books referred back further and further, until I was reading about events of two thousand years ago. It took a year or two for me to figure out that this was the biblical period, and I decided to go right to the source. I also began corresponding at that time with an Israeli pen pal.*

I bought a Bible and ripped out the New Testament section. The way I understood it, the Old Testament was a historical account, and the New Testament was a religious document, and I knew from my father that organized religion led to no good. I don't really know why I tore it out. I hid the Bible in my room because I was worried my choice of reading material might upset my father. The next logical step was for me to learn Hebrew so I could read the text in the original, so I found an old Jewish man who was teaching two other students: a young Jewish girl, and a man studying for the priesthood. I suggested to my Israeli pen pal that we switch to Hebrew, which we did, even though a three-page letter from her would take me five hours to decipher.

By age sixteen and a half, I had read the Old Testament all the way through six or seven times. It's hard to explain but I started to see a pattern in it. I mean, I started to see the hand of God. It was a slow process, but it became apparent to me that there was a metaphysical dimension to what I first thought of as only stories.

Holland sends draft notices to its young men a year before their induction date. There is a response form with all manner of questions, one of which is, whom do you want as your chaplain: priest, minister, rabbi, or humanist. Yossi checked off "rabbi." Soon after he returned the form, the rabbi invited to his house the inductees who had checked him off. He was a little surprised to find a non-Jew among the group, but it did not bother him. Yossi explained that he chose a rabbi because he had no feelings for Christianity, but was interested in the State of Israel.

Over the next half year, Yossi felt more and more strongly that he wanted to be part of the Jewish people. He read whatever he could get his hands on, and decided he wanted to observe the commandments. He had never heard of conversion; he had no idea it was possible to change your religious affiliation. He just knew he wanted to practice Judaism. The rabbi tried to discourage him; Judaism does not seek converts. Judaism holds that there is no need or requirement for the entire world to be Jewish. The requirement is for everyone to behave ethically. This is what the rabbi explained to Yossi, but he would not be put off. The rabbi was not convinced that Yossi would end up converting, but he prepared a study program for him.

One day I was in my room practicing the Hebrew Grace after Meals text when my mother walked in, looked over my shoulder at the page I was reading, and started reading it with me. It was the first time she had seen Hebrew since before the war. I didn't react, because I didn't connect it to her being Jewish. That was not a possibility in my mind. When she caught herself, she stopped short and sputtered that she had been an au pair to a Jewish family and had to learn Hebrew in order to help the children with their homework. I really thought nothing of it.

Once in the army, I asked to be stationed near a kosher facility, and the army put me near a Jewish home for the aged. Twice a month I would spend a half day studying with my rabbi. After a year, I decided to convert. I told my mother first because I expected less resistance from her than from my father because of his views on religion. She didn't say anything, and we all talked about it for a bit. It seemed I was right. It was harder for my father to have a child who wanted to be religious in whatever form. But true to his tolerant outlook, he didn't challenge my decision.

I spent most weekends at home, and went to services at the local synagogue where I would join the hazzan *for lunch and spend the afternoon with his family, studying the Bible. It was a wonderful time for me. Until then, I had only been reading, but those weekends were the first time I actually* experienced *Judaism, lived it in a community setting. I scheduled an inpatient circumcision, and two weeks before my conversion ceremony, I told my parents that I was about to convert. At that point, when she saw that it was truly going to happen, my mother sat me down and told me her story.*

It was a great, great shock. I was absolutely numb. By that time, I knew about the Holocaust and I was horrified to find out that my mother had suffered the loss of her entire family. I heard her words, but it took a long time until the meaning sank in. She explained why she left Judaism, which I, of course, understood. She made me promise not to tell anyone we knew. To this day, she tells people that the reason I live in Israel is because I married an Israeli girl.

The one person I did tell was my rabbi. He, too, was shocked. He researched the archives and found the documents tracing my ancestry and confirming my Jewish status. He likened my story to a tiny oven pilot light that's always on but waiting to be fueled into a blazing flame.

Yossi's brother, a year and a half younger, found the family history interesting, but it had no impact on his lifestyle. He became engaged, and, after a good few months, realized that his fiancée's mother is Jewish. He is married now, still living in Holland, and has a son to whom he gave an Israeli name. He and his wife are raising their son to identify with Jewish culture but not with any religion.

After his army service, Yossi moved to Israel where he met his wife in 1974.

As my studies continued, my mother would sometimes read with me. I could see the Hebrew prayers and tunes were awakening happy memories for her, memories from before the war. Ten years ago, on a visit to us, she held the candle in our Saturday-night ceremony as we said goodbye to the Sabbath, and my father must have seen the same look on her face that I did because he took her aside and told her that if he lost her to religion, that would be a hard blow for him. I think that's why she hasn't expressed more interest, even though I suspect she would like to.

I don't ask my mother questions about the past because I know it's hard for her to talk, but time is passing and I really wanted to know the names of her family members, so I asked both my parents if we could make a family tree the way my wife just did, and only last week she told me the names of her parents and siblings, which I shared with the Holocaust documentation center at Yad VaShem in Jerusalem so there would be a memorial of them.

Yossi is eager for his story to be told, but he respects his mother's privacy and anxiety too much to allow use of the family name. He lives a life thoroughly permeated by Jewishness and, though that creates differences between them, has taught his children to regard their Dutch grandparents with respect and affection, much the way his father taught him to allow for differences among people.

Yossi took it in stride when his mother read Hebrew over his shoulder, as though it were the most natural thing in the world for a person to start speaking in tongues. Perhaps he had an inner voice telling him not to ask uncomfortable questions. In separate interviews, the three Landmann sisters recounted to me the same type of incident.

The Landmann parents are German-Jewish Holocaust survivors. Mrs. Landmann was raised as a Christian by her assimilated Jewish parents. According to the Nuremberg Laws, though, she and her family were Jewish, and they had to flee in 1938. Mr. Landmann was the sole survivor of his family, which was deported when he was seventeen. His sister and parents probably ended up in Auschwitz, and he was sent to a labor camp, from which he escaped. He lived underground in Berlin until he made his way to Switzerland and, after the war, to New York. The couple met in New York City, married, and had their three girls baptized. Mrs. Landmann attended the Presbyterian Church, while Mr. Landmann declared himself an agnostic. "I worship the tennis ball," he used to joke to his daughters on Sunday mornings.

The Landmanns had longtime friends in Maine whom they would all visit once a year. This family was also German-born, but they lived as Jews. One year, when the girls were preteens, they visited the Jewish family in April. Having arrived on the eve of Passover, they were invited to join in the Seder, the ceremonial evening meal. The host distributed a Haggadah (script for the Seder proceedings) to each person at the table. The girls looked on as their father, Mr. Landmann, sang the Passover songs in Hebrew, as though he had been celebrating the Jewish holiday all his life!

"We thought he was so smart. Isn't Daddy amazing, we said, all he has to do is *look* at a foreign language, and he picks it up right away!" It turned out that this "family friend" was the bosom buddy with whom Mr. Landmann had spent his wartime years running from the Nazis. Not one of the daughters questioned her father's instantaneous command of a foreign language, though they each recalled it.

Survivors of the Holocaust did not want their children to suffer the torments they had endured. To protect them, some took the evasive action of eliminating all traces of Jewishness from the family. While they may have succeeded in erasing their genealogy, they were not always able to avoid those behavior patterns that accrue to a survivor of catastrophic persecution.

Janos Nanasi was born in Hungary just after the war to a nonpracticing Catholic father and a Jewish mother who had survived Auschwitz. There were clues to his mother's religious affiliation, but they were meaningless to Janos, who lived under a government that discouraged any form of religious education. His mother used to light yahrzeit (Jewish anniversary of death) candles for her first husband, and her mother and daughter. She baked challah, the traditional Sabbath braided bread, every Friday. She served matzo during Passover week. Not one of those items by itself was unusual enough to arouse Janos's curiosity.

When I was ten, we were playing in the street and a guy came over and asked us our parents' names. When he heard my mother's maiden name, he said, so you must be Jewish, too. I thought I was going to die of shame. But I knew it couldn't be true because my father's mother went to church every day, so I figured the guy must be crazy. I never mentioned it to my mother. That summer, in camp, when I showered with the other boys, I discovered I looked different from them. I didn't know why but, again, I didn't ask my parents about it. In high school I noticed that my mother would get letters from Israel. I asked her who they were from, but she wouldn't answer.

Even when I made close Jewish friends in college and figured out that my mother must be Jewish, I still didn't confront her, but the discovery was making an impression on me. I took a trip to France during my college years and bought a Star of David necklace. That was my "coming out." A few years later I married a non-Jewish woman. We had two children, and decided to leave Hungary in order to raise them as Jews and give them greater opportunities. Both my parents were supportive. My wife, from whom I am divorced, got a Reform conversion. The children converted of their own accord when they were older.

Nine years ago, I moved to Texas and got involved with the Holocaust center. The truth is, I needed cheap therapy. I joined their writing project and recorded oral histories of survivors. By that time, I felt the need to know my mother's story, so I interviewed her. She wrote her story in Hungarian and I translated it. That's when I found out I wasn't an only child. And I found out my father was her second husband. And that she had survived a death camp.

She told me she was from an Orthodox Jewish family. She married at age nineteen. Her husband was taken away by the Nazis shortly after, and she and her baby and her parents were shipped off to Auschwitz. When they got there, her mother was holding the baby and the two of them were sent to the gas chambers as soon as they got off the train. My mother and her father were assigned to work details, and managed to stay alive until the Liberation.

After the war, she found out her husband had been killed. She married my father in 1952, a year after her father had moved to Israel. When he heard about her marriage to a non-Jew, he declared her dead. But when he found out that she had me ritually circumcised, he started corresponding with her. That explains the letters I used to see from Israel.

I know my mother loves me because she cares about me and she feeds me all the time. Eating was a big deal in our family. But there were no hugs, no "I love you"s. Maybe she was afraid to get close because she lost everyone in the camps. We didn't have a loving, expressive relationship. I did the same with my wife. And with my children. I just didn't know how to express affection. I've worked very hard the last few years to overcome that problem, and I think I've succeeded with my children and with my new wife.

I started out at the Holocaust Center as a volunteer, but as soon as there was a job opening there, I left my job in hotel management and grabbed it. I love going to work. There hasn't been one day that I've regretted my choice. I'm proud of my accomplishments, especially that I was able to raise my children as Jews. It feels good to be Jewish.

Rose Zabriski carried my address in her wallet for ten months before sending me a postcard that read, "It's probably too late but I was born in Poland, raised Catholic, immigrated to the US in '59 at age seven, and learned at 22 (the night before my Roman Catholic wedding) that both my parents were Holocaust survivors and that all of our family is Jewish."

I had already written this chapter, but Rose's postcard intrigued me. For one thing, the postcard was a nighttime winter scene of a snowbound house with trees all around and what had to be Christmas lights adorning the house. The house itself is dark, and there are icicles hanging from the roof, but one of the trees is radiant, as though it were illuminated from within.

I found that postcard to be representative of Rose herself. It was not until midway through our hour and a half conversation that she revealed what a dark past she had come from, yet her voice was luminous and her outlook radiated warmth.

My mother was from a non-practicing Jewish family. They were landed gentry in Lvov, with servants and horses. Her father died of kidney disease before the war. Her brother went off to fight and never returned. He probably died in concentration camp. My mother went into hiding with her mother. At one point, it became too dangerous for them to stay together, so they separated. That was when my grandmother was caught and shot. My mother never got over it. She spent the rest of the war hidden by Ukrainians in their hayloft.

My father had a similar history. He and his father wanted to flee Warsaw, but his mother and sister couldn't believe the Nazis would hurt women and children, so they refused to budge. My father and grandfather left without them. To this day, my father says he doesn't understand how they made that decision. Of course, he would have been killed if he had stayed. His mother committed suicide when she realized her mistake. The sister, who I'm named after, escaped from the ghetto and went back to her neighborhood. The next-door neighbor hid her, but she soon died of an advanced case of tuberculosis.

After the war, my parents met in medical school. That was when my mother convinced my father to convert. She was afraid to be Jewish. My father figured, God is God, and it doesn't really matter which church you're in, so he went along with it. I was born in 1952. They sent me to Catholic school and we all went to church together. But they must have had mixed feelings because when my younger brother was five, they had him circumcised. We moved to the States in 1959.

I met my first husband after graduation. Before the wedding, my mother made it clear to my father's sister that her husband wasn't welcome because he looked too Jewish, and my mother didn't want to risk exposure. Maybe it was out of revenge that my aunt told me the night before my wedding that my parents were Jewish Holocaust survivors. I remember asking my father, why didn't you tell me? And he said that it was never the right time. But he said that when I graduated he would send me around the world to meet my family. And he made good on that promise. When I got my Ph.D., after my first divorce, I spent three months in Israel and nine months going from country to country meeting relatives.

At first, the idea of being Jewish didn't mean anything to me because I didn't know anything about it. Later, as I read Holocaust novels like Exodus and Mila 18, it became more and more meaningful. My brother is into Eastern religions. He turned me on to Buddhism and meditation. I still don't know a whole lot about Judaism. I think of it as a culture, not a religion.

It's only in the last few years that I can tell people my parents are survivors. Their suffering was so immense that I felt I didn't deserve any *sympathy I might get from telling. All that sympathy really belongs to them.*

My mother had classic survivor's guilt. She had multiple sclerosis, which she didn't treat. It was part of her self-punishment. In family therapy, when she was asked why she never defended me against my father's beatings, she said, what beatings? She was in total denial.

My father was violent with me until halfway through college. Generally, he was warmer than my mother, but he had episodic flare-ups. I knew I was loved because there was nothing they wouldn't do for me. But my mother was so emotionally unavailable. Maybe she couldn't deal with having a daughter because she never dealt with losing her mother. She never grieved or talked about it. She'd go into a trance. Maybe she never forgave herself for separating from her mother.

They would give me the silent treatment for weeks after a beating. I never learned how to express anger, and that was a problem in my marriage. I've worked on it since then, and I think I've learned a lot. I'm a super kids' therapist. I love children, but I don't have any of my own. I was so aware of how much damage parents can do that I was frightened away.

Rose and Janos have achieved an extraordinary degree of healing through hard work in therapy. Janos has remarried, and he and his wife, Kathryn, live as observant, Orthodox Jews. Neither Rose nor Janos expressed any bitterness. On the contrary, they talked about forgiveness and understanding. Both spoke with gentleness and a positive attitude. Their parents had survived the death camps, and so had they.

There are individuals who were raised so far removed from their origins, or even in opposition to their origins, that to discover their roots is a chilling disappointment. Rose talked about regarding Judaism as a culture as opposed to a religion. For Denny Jacobson and Pete Weicz, learning of their Jewishness cast them into a spiritual isolation.

Denny has a distinguished European accent, and speaks in a calm, even tone. He was very open, and has obviously given a great deal of thought to the convoluted path his life has taken.

I was born in Berlin in 1939. My father was a technical writer. He had to resign from the technical writers' guild in 1936 because he wasn't an

Aryan. We moved to England when I was three months old. My parents never had me circumcised but they did have me baptized. When we moved, they left all vestiges of Judaism behind. They even dropped the h *from Jacobsohn in an effort to anglicize the name.*

My father's two sisters married German non-Jews and moved to England. One had a husband who stayed in Germany working in the Underground trying to save Jews. He was turned in to the Gestapo and committed suicide. Both aunts adopted Christianity and still live in England. My mother's brother moved to Israel in the mid-1930s. He's a secular Jew. His son lives not far from me. I've seen them both several times.

Our family didn't really practice anything, but we celebrated Christmas. I went to a very Anglican private school (which we called public school in Britain). We began each day with prayers in the chapel. I was very aware of my parents' German roots. My parents had pronounced German accents. It was extremely uncomfortable to be German in England just after the war. They never discussed why they left.

In my late teens I found my parents' passports and my birth certificate. They were issued under the Nazi regime and had been stamped "Mosaiche." That's when I figured out we were Jewish. It wasn't much of an issue for me because by then I had become disillusioned with Christianity. Like any teenager, I put as much effort as I could into trying to assimilate into the surrounding culture. My sister, who is three years older, went to a girls' school where she had the same problems I did. She just wanted to fit in, and had to overcome the stigma of having German-speaking parents. It was a difficult period for both of us.

My mother died in 1991, and my father in 1983. I've been doing a lot of thinking. I'm more comfortable and familiar with Christian rites. I've only been to temple maybe two or three times in my life. I have friends in the Jewish community through my involvement in second-generation activities. I've pretty much decided not to go back to any form of practicing Christianity. I subscribe to the idea of monotheism but it would be a sham for me to call myself Jewish because I don't follow any of the rituals. I'm interested in Jewish history and thought. I've been to Israel once but I have mixed feelings about it because I feel strongly that church and state should be separate. I may go again next year.

I went to second-generation support groups on and off for about three years, beginning in 1993. We share issues like early development of self-

reliance and parenting our parents. Children of survivors have a constant feeling of insecurity. From age six, apart from food and clothing, I had to make decisions for myself. I intuited the need not to bother my parents.

Fundamentally, I feel there were two major splits in my life in areas that are "givens" for most people: nationality and religion. Many times people ask me, where were you born, and I feel I have to be evasive. I'm ambivalent about divulging my German roots. And the religious issue is also cloudy for me. Like anyone, I have a need for spirituality, but how to express it? That's why I'm drawn to the ideas of Joseph Campbell or Rosicrucianism.[2] *My sister is into early spiritual beliefs, like shamanism.*

Most of the people in the second-generation group are American-born. They have a national identity and a Jewish identity. I had a somewhat different agenda: I'm kind of a survivor and a child of survivors at one and the same time. Because my parents are German and not overtly Jewish, I am nationally identified with the atrocities. Yet, because they were born Jewish, I'm also a victim.

Denny was stuck in a spiritual no man's land. His primary familiarity was with Christian ritual. That was, after all, a daily and integral part of his elementary school education. And yet, he was affected enough by the knowledge of his Jewish background to participate in second-generation groups. It must have been an effort, because those groups are comprised primarily of children raised in homes that are clearly Jewish in identity and culture. He had to have felt very much the foreigner.

Denny put me in touch with Pete, who, while younger, suffered the same feelings of alienation.

My parents survived the war by hiding, but their families were killed. Those Hungarian Jews who didn't perish in the camps were killed by Nazi sympathizers toward the end of the war. That happened to my grandparents. Luckily, my father saw a physician he knew and asked him to say he was the Christian maid's son. It worked, but his parents were taken to a concentration camp and died when it was bombed.

Two months before the Russian siege, my mother's family was marched to a central area. She told her father they should slip away, but he couldn't abandon the rest of the family, so she escaped alone. She rejoined her mother in a hiding place. It turned out her father was put in a concentration camp. Her mother bribed a guard and got him out, but he was beaten to death later on. A physician at a Catholic nursing home offered my mother a hiding place, which is where she lived out the rest of the war.

My parents came to Canada in 1949, and to the U.S. in 1964. In Canada they decided to convert, but they weren't comfortable with Catholicism, so I grew up Lutheran. We celebrated holidays, I went to Sunday school, my mother took us to church. In the States, my elementary school in White Plains was 85 percent Jewish. I thought I was the only Christian kid in the school.

When I was twelve or thirteen, my brother asked my parents why our relatives in Montreal are Jewish, and they decided to tell us the truth. We were in the kitchen. I was pretty surprised. I always felt that they kept it from us to protect us. I have two brothers. Neither of us is circumcised. It's not a common procedure in Canada.

I had some feelings of embarrassment when I found out. I've gone through a lot since then. There's some anti-Semitism in me. I'm scared to be perceived as Jewish. I've always shied away from having Jewish friends. I'm just now starting to date a Jewish girl for the first time in my life. I've dated mostly Irish Catholics. One of my brothers is getting divorced from a non-Jewish woman. The other is not married.

After I started speaking about my Jewish background, I felt more integrated. I feel some guilt about keeping it a secret. The way I saw it was: a secret is something you equate with something shameful, so being Jewish must be shameful to some extent; otherwise it wouldn't be a secret.

I have mixed feelings about telling. After all, it's still a family secret. Sometimes I thought I was being disingenuous not telling people. I actually subjected myself to more anti-Semitism as a result of not telling, because people felt free to make prejudiced remarks in my presence. That was disturbing. I would think, wow, now I really *don't want them to know I'm Jewish.*

One of my worst memories is from when I was seventeen, and a close friend spewed anti-Semitic comments. I guess I acted defensive, because he called me later and said his mother suggested I might have some Jewish relatives, which I denied. I've always felt bad about not telling him the truth.

My father never went to church. He had mixed feelings about the decision to convert, and sent mixed messages. He assumed everybody knew anyway. It was problematic for me because for a while I was getting physically sick from the tension of it.

I don't go to church or to temple. I don't feel any need to become Jewish. Talking is cathartic. I'm getting more comfortable with who I am now. I was invited to a Seder this year. Not to sound arrogant, but it didn't mean much of anything to me. It was kind of neat, but it felt foreign.

I traveled to Budapest two years ago to understand my history better, but I'm not excessively curious. I met some relatives in Hungary. There aren't many left. Most converted to Christianity.

Denny and I were the two non-Jews in the second-generation group. We can't relate when the others throw off Yiddish phrases. We're outsiders. I don't feel a strong sense of identity with any group. Certain life choices I've made are probably consistent with this background of the Holocaust. For example, I'm a lawyer and a teacher, and I try to be open-minded. I speak out against injustice.

I have no extended family. Growing up with immigrant parents, I never felt quite a part of things. I have feelings of being marginalized. I'm not part of either the Jewish community or the Christian community.

Denny talked about seeing himself as both a survivor and a child of survivors. That claim can surely be made by Anna M., who was born in Bulgaria in 1939 to a Bulgarian (Christian Eastern Orthodox) mother and a Catholic father, whose mother was Italian and father Hungarian. A few years before Anna was born, her paternal grandparents divorced. Her grandfather subsequently married his ex-wife's cousin, inciting a *Grande Scandale* in the family. The couple moved back to Hungary and had a daughter. The grandfather became pretty much *persona non grata*, and Anna didn't hear about him as she grew up.

In 1946, at the conclusion of the Second World War, after serving a stretch in a concentration camp by invitation of the Communist Party in Bulgaria, my father and I (me being on his passport) had to leave Bulgaria because foreigners were all expelled. My mother, a Bulgarian national, had to figure her own way to get out.

We went to Italy where we stayed in a D.P. camp near Naples, and signed up to immigrate as displaced persons. My mother joined us a year later. I was sent to a Catholic boarding school in Rome while my parents searched for work. When our number finally was called in 1951, we were sent to a processing camp in Bremenhaven, Germany. Even though the war had been over for several years, we were greeted by German guards with Doberman pinschers and German shepherds, to make sure that nobody got off the train at an unscheduled stop. To this day I break out in a sweat at the sight of those breeds.

We stayed in that camp for less than a month. There was a lot of despair. There were suicides. Sometimes only one member of a family was not approved—maybe because of an unobtainable document or an old T.B. scar (healed, but there nevertheless)—and the entire family would be refused entry into their "new country."

We were a very mixed group. Christian, Jewish, and Protestant charities sponsored our passage to the U.S.A. I was twelve when we boarded the boat. My mother took ill and we had a terrible storm, so she was bedridden in a military hammock. There was an outbreak of some children's disease, but since I had had them all (there were no vaccines), I worked in the infirmary and was allowed to bring her food.

In the mornings, on my way to the infirmary, I would pass a group of Jewish men praying on deck with their prayers shawls on . . . and in a sense this is where my story begins. Somehow I knew that these were my people.

Like many newly arrived families, we immersed ourselves in the business of making a living and fitting in. I always had the feeling that we had Jewish family or were Jewish ourselves, but I was not able to actually ask the question. When I did ask my mother about it during her last illness in 1979, her answer was, "No, we have no Jewish relatives." Then, when I started working on our genealogy, my father also denied having any Jewish relatives, but the way he answered always raised more questions.

He died in 1987, but I continued my family history research. When it came to my paternal grandfather, I always hit a dead end. He was a second lieutenant in Hungary during the First World War, and there should have been some record. At long last I consulted my only older living relative in the States—an aunt residing in a senior citizens' complex in Brooklyn. After ascertaining that I had no animosity toward the

Jewish people, she hesitantly disclosed that my grandfather had been Jewish. She had names and birth dates of his parents, and names of his four brothers, one of whom had a peach farm near Budapest where my dad spent many of his working vacations. In 1921, my grandfather changed his last name from the obviously Jewish Oesterreicher to the ethnically generic Ottai. I went through my father's documents and sure enough, his name changed, too, that year.

This disclosure was a great relief for me. I had felt crazy all those years, thinking I was Jewish but getting no confirmation. I wrote to my father's stepsister in New Zealand and she confirmed that her father had been Jewish but secular, and had died at the end of World War II.

I am convinced my father never told my mother that his father was Jewish. It is rather sad that the rest of the family knew and we didn't. As it was, there was much religious strife in our family between the Catholics and the Bulgarian Orthodox. Eventually my parents divorced.

I have always had a strong belief in God, but something was very lacking in the religions I was familiar with. Now I felt free to find out what Judaism was about. I have studied on my own for the past three years. I live in a town of about four thousand, but I have a good Jewish library and access to the Internet. After many rejections, I finally found a rabbi who will work with me on my conversion. At twenty-six, my daughter is also showing interest. My husband studies with me, but has not yet committed himself.

Last Yom Kippur [Jewish Day of Atonement] I flew to Anchorage, which is 250 miles from where I live, to attend services. The service came naturally to me, and the Kol Nidre prayer was strangely familiar. It's hard to explain. Before, I never felt that I fit in. Now I feel complete, like this is home.

A year after our initial correspondence, Anna wrote to me again. In the "Topic" section of the email address, she wrote, "Miracle" because she regards it as no less than miraculous that at age fifty-nine, in a small town in Alaska, she finally found a rabbi who agreed to teach her and then to convert her.

He gathered a beit din [Jewish tribunal], and a Jewish woman to witness the immersion. We have no mikvah [ritualarium] here on the Kenai

Peninsula. He gave me the prayers to recite. We found a creek deep enough (all glacial here so it was rather on the chilly side) and now I am a Jewish woman with a Jewish name.

Escape from Nazi Germany did not ensure escape from the damaging effects of displacement and dispersal. People who were uprooted from their native cultures suffered from the disruption of normal family life. This damage often extended to the next generation as well.

Even though Carol M. was born in Boston, her life's twists and turns were a direct result of Hitler's policies. I met Carol in a small hotel in Jerusalem, where she lives. She climbed the thirty steps to the lobby despite what I could see was crippling arthritic pain. The pain had etched itself onto her face, but she was gaily dressed in a colorful outfit that set off her deep black hair. As she spoke, I caught glimpses of the girl she had been behind the grown woman she is now.

My mother was raised Jewish but not religious in Breslau. In 1937, after the Nuremberg Laws were enacted, she met my father, a Lutheran psychiatrist, in the hospital where she worked as a nurse. She converted in order to marry him. I have the family Bible, which records her baptism the same day as their wedding.

They decided to move to Boston when life in Germany became untenable. Because of the anti-Semitism in Boston, my mother decided to hide her origins. I was born there in 1939, and they had me baptized. My godmother took me to Sunday school every week. My parents didn't go to church, but I became very religious. My father died when I was seven. My younger sister was only one and a half. She was never baptized.

My mother had nobody in America, so she decided to move us to Palestine, where she had two sisters. I remember going to my aunt's kibbutz wearing my crucifix. When my uncle saw it, he ripped it off my neck and replaced it with a Star of David without any explanation. That was a traumatic moment for me. Nobody told me what was going on.

They sent me to boarding school here. Then during the 1947 Arab riots, my mother took us back to America, but I had forgotten how to speak English. She sent me to boarding school there, too. I was placed with a Christian American family until I was nine. But my mother couldn't adapt, and we went back to Tel Aviv for good. In all, I went to first grade four times, twice in America and twice in Israel.

During my formative years I was Christian. Then my world was shattered. I missed my church, my religion, my godmother. It was a terrible time for me. I was wild with grief and rage. And furious that nobody ever explained what was going on. My mother is buried in Germany. We never had a single conversation about her background.

Once we moved back to Israel, it took me four or five years to settle in. At first, Hebrew was impossible for me. Later, I took to it like lightning. Now I read the Bible and commentaries in the original for my research. I'm a trained nurse but I study art history. My concentration is periods of transition, like the Greco-Roman, Judeo-Christian and medieval Renaissance periods—which makes sense, given my background.

I married my ex-husband at age twenty-one. My three children identify with the Jewish social traditions. One daughter married an Irish Catholic. They live in Oregon. He converted. Now he's the only observant Jew in the family! He goes to synagogue and they keep a kosher home.

I love Israel. Every stone here is meaningful. My kids take it for granted. I raised them to be patriotic. My sons served in combat units. One was stationed in Lebanon. Now they want to get out of reserve duty, which saddens me.

Myself, I feel Jewish. I observe the holidays as social events. I found it scandalous when the Bible was made optional instead of mandatory in Israeli schools, and I'm amazed I feel that way. I absolutely identify now as a Jew.

Carol had endured many losses—the comfort of her church, separation from her beloved godmother, the death of her father, the absence of her mother during the boarding school years. But once she and her mother and sister moved back to Israel to stay, she had a much more stable environment. Her schooling also normalized. She made lasting friends in class and in the neighborhood—Jewish Israeli friends. All these factors doubtless helped her gain her equilibrium and put down roots. In that sense, she is the embodiment of a survivor.

Dear Barbara,

Pawel was my guide when I toured Krakow and Birkenau. He is a stu-

dent at the Jagiellonian University, whose paternal Jewish grandfather was able to avoid detection by the Nazis and lived as a non-Jew the rest of his life. After he died, the family was told this secret.

As we were walking through the Birkenau death camp, we came across three local kids playing there and disturbing some of the rubble. Pawel got very upset and chased the kids off. He then told me that when he first visited Birkenau as an elementary school student (which Pawel thought was much too young), most of the kids played but he cried. Today, now that he knows his grandfather and probably his grandmother were Jewish, he understands his reaction. Since learning this four years ago, this young man, Pawel, has been keenly interested in his Jewish heritage.

I told him about your project and he is eager to correspond with you.

Sincerely, Mark

Some Jews managed to survive Nazism under the pretense that they were Christians. Today there is a resurgence of Judaism among Polish youth who have discovered they are of Jewish descent. Like crypto-Jews, the newly Jewish Poles are viewed askance in certain quarters either because some lack definitive proof of their ancestry or because they are suspected of trying to access the benefits extended by Jewish or Israeli relief organizations. Skepticism aside, there is a corpus of Polish youngsters just now finding out they are the children or grandchildren of Jews who passed as non-Jews during the Holocaust. Survivors on their deathbeds are confessing their religious affiliation to their children as are superannuated foster parents—the non-Jewish neighbors who saved these children by raising them as their own. With their last breath, many are revealing to these grown children or grandchildren their Jewish parentage. Lamentably, the children have few or no remaining relatives to fill in the information gaps. Such a one is Pawel.

Dear Mrs. Barbara Kessel:

I am very sorry that it took me so long to write you but right now I am in the middle of exams term at my university. Maybe I write you some words about myself. I am studying at the Jagiellonian University in Krakow. My main field is Political Science/International Relations.

As a teenager I never was an anti-Semite. I was interested in everything what was concerned to the Jewish people. In high school we had a lot of fights about Jews. I always tried to show people in my class that Jews were the same people as us.

From that time I wanted to know something more. Unfortunately my grandparents died several years ago and I could not talk to them. I found that my great-grandfather was Jewish.

My parents have never brought pressure to bear on me to go to the church. The truth is that I was raised without any religion. They were very liberal.

I am thinking very seriously about converting to the Judaism. I made my decision that I want to do it, but right now there is not time to prepare. I will write you some more details later because besides my study I also have a job and not a lot of time. I am sorry for that.

Yours sincerely, Pawel.

The majority of people I interviewed found out about their ancestry through a "breach in security." Usually, there were branches of the family who did not try to hide or subvert the truth. Those branches were either sworn not to divulge the information, or they were simply cut off from contact. The usual scenario was that a relative would "slip" and reveal the family secret. This is what happened in Rosemary Frei's family.

My mother's mother was born in Amsterdam. We can trace her family tree back twelve generations. They were Ashkenazic [Germanic] Jews, devoutly secular since the French Revolution. My mother didn't even know she was Jewish until she was nine, when another child used her ethnicity as a taunt against her. Her father was not Jewish and was from an aristocratic Dutch family.

My grandparents and my mother migrated to Indonesia, a Dutch colony, in 1936, when my mother was three. My grandfather was desperate for work; many Dutch went there to earn a living. My grandfather accepted a position as a sales representative for a factory that made wrappings out of materials such as paper, cardboard, and sheet metal. In March 1942, the Japanese occupied Indonesia and my grandfather was placed in a POW camp immediately. He had fought in the Dutch army. In January 1944, my mother and her mother were also put in a Japanese concentration camp. My grandfather was killed in September 1944. He was being carried in a Japanese cargo ship jammed beyond the rafters with POWs and forced laborers, when it was torpedoed by a British submarine. My mother and her mother only found out a year later.

They couldn't get out of Indonesia until 1946, because the countrymen rebelled against the Dutch occupation, and my mother and grandmother were surrounded by the fighting. They went back to Holland. My widowed grandmother married her late husband's first cousin, and they came here to Canada when my mother was fifteen. My mother would have preferred to stay in Holland. It was very hard for her because there were so many transitions. My mother had herself baptized in an effort to fit into Canadian Christian society. My mother's mother decided that she would never tell anyone in Canada that she was Jewish. In fact, she joined the church, and in the 1980s she converted to Christianity. But my grandmother looked very Jewish—and my father knew my mother's family was Jewish.

He was born in Prague to a Catholic family, but stopped practicing when he was thirteen. Before my parents got married, my mother's mother told them never to tell their kids that they are Jewish. I can only guess that this was because she did not know much about Judaism and what she did know was that being Jewish can be life-threatening. My parents had two boys and three girls. I'm the youngest. We were raised "Christian Lite." We went to church until I was five, and my family still celebrates Christmas and has an Easter dinner.

In 1982, my oldest brother went to Holland to complete a year as a law clerk. We still have family there, and one of my mother's cousins mentioned to my brother that we're Jewish through my grandmother. My brother was surprised and upset that his grandmother, with whom he had a very close relationship, had withheld this important information from him and his siblings. When he came home and confronted my mother, she had to tell all of us. She told us one by one that my grandmother had left Judaism behind in her young childhood and that she had made them promise never to tell their children.

When I found out I was Jewish, I didn't care. Five years later, however, at the end of 1989, I began to have spiritual yearnings. I visited Anglican and Catholic churches but they didn't "do anything" for me. Then I remembered my mother had told me I'm Jewish, and I looked up synagogues in the telephone directory of Calgary, Alberta, where I was living at the time. I happened to call the Conservative synagogue and the rabbi invited me to his Roots class for converts. I went to a class and liked what I heard—it made sense intellectually and also appealed to my heart and soul. After the class, the rabbi took me into his study and said, "If you decide to follow a Jewish life, you'll have to keep kosher and marry Jewish." I had just walked in the door!

I started going to the Conservative synagogue regularly. It was very daunting at first to go to a place where the Hebrew-language service and customs were unfamiliar, but the people were very friendly. And I kept going to the Roots class. I slowly took on more and more practices, like observing the Sabbath. That's why it was so disconcerting when the rabbi started to push me away, as Judaism does with potential converts. I switched to a Reform congregation for a while to check it out, but soon went back to the Conservative shul [synagogue]. At the end of 1991, I joined a group from London, Ontario (where my parents lived), for a three-week tour of Israel and Egypt. Israel didn't feel like home, but I was glad I went.

Two years later, my mother and I went to Holland. It was her idea, because in Israel I had found records at the Yad VaShem Holocaust Museum of her grandfather's being taken to Auschwitz. My mother was very moved by that and wanted to find out more about her family's past. Her mother knew more, of course, but she refused to discuss it.

When we were in Amsterdam, we found the house my great-grandfather had lived in. The current residents remembered him. He was taken away in 1942. One of our extended family members gave us a postcard that my great-grandfather and his second wife had written to a good friend from a train to a transit camp on the way to Auschwitz. It said, "We're resigned to our fate. Say goodbye to everyone." My mother has that postcard now. We also found my great-grandmother's grave in an Orthodox Jewish cemetery outside of Amsterdam.

We also asked for and received an official letter from the main Jewish organization in Holland attesting to the fact that my mother's mother's mother is buried in a Jewish cemetery. I presented this document to my rabbi (by then I had joined an Orthodox synagogue), who in turn showed it to the rabbinic court in charge of conversions of the [Orthodox] Rabbinical Council of America. That court ruled that, while I am

Jewish by birth, I had to go to the mikvah [ritual bath] because I had been baptized and so had my mother, and thus I had to take a concrete step to renounce my past and rejoin the Jewish fold. I am slowly learning biblical Hebrew, and I do a lot of studying. Since the beginning of my long journey back to my Jewish roots I have felt a strong and direct connection to God. I also have a strong idea of where I stand in terms of hashkafa [philosophy]. I categorize myself as Centrist Orthodox.

My family is on the whole supportive of my decision to embrace Orthodox Judaism. My mother is particularly positive—I think I've been able to be an agent for her to learn more about some of the secrets that her family harbored for years and to think more about what her understanding of God is and what her relationship is to Her/Him.

My grandmother went to church regularly until the end of her life in the summer of 1977. She said that she was too old to change. She was a strong character. She and I were in the car one day and I took out my prayerbook to recite the traveler's prayer. When my grandmother heard the Hebrew words, she reflexively burst out with "Sh'ma Yisrael" [Hear O Israel], the fundamental Jewish declaration of faith. That was an affirming and very powerful experience for me.

When my mother and I went to Holland, Grandmother wrote to our relatives there warning them not to tell us about what happened during the war. They did anyway. I'm glad they did. I think it's better for me—and all of my family members—to understand where we came from so that we can face the future as whole and healthy people.

Once Rosemary's mother shared her history with her children, she became supportive of her daughter's quest, going so far as to accompany her to her European birthplace to research their family history. Rosemary's journey carried her not only eastward, but backwards in chronology and genealogy until she arrived full circle at her newly revealed heritage and encamped there.

Photographer Zigy Kaluzny found the news that he was Jewish grounding. It gave him a sense of place, it fixed the coordinates of his identity in time and space. His parents had married and divorced each other twice, and it could well be that Zigy was seeking the feeling of stability that an ethnic history could provide.

Dear Barbara:

My father was a Russian Jew. His mother and five sisters disappeared in the Holocaust but he survived because he was finishing medical school in Italy where he met my mother, a Hungarian Protestant. I was born there in 1947, and we came to the States in 1951. Although my parents divorced early in my life, my mother chose to live in a Jewish area of Chicago. I was raised Protestant, but the religion never spoke to me. I don't have any religious (as opposed to spiritual) interests. All I know is that I always felt more natural and comfortable, at home, with Jews than around non-Jews. I had always assumed it was more of an intellectual connection than anything else.

Some years ago, I noted to my mother that it was interesting that of the three sisters in her family, two had married Jewish men. My mother then told me that HER *mother had been Jewish and had converted before marriage because Grandfather was an anti-Semite. I was profoundly moved, as I am even as I write this. Suddenly I had the sense of being connected to a world, a place in history, a people, that I have never experienced (normal in children of divorced parents—mine had been married and divorced from each other twice). To me, Judaism is a culture, not just a religion, and it gives me a place to belong.*

Zigy had never been involved with a Jewish woman, but he clearly had a strong sense of connection. He has just turned fifty, and has met a Jewish woman he finds attractive. Either the milestone birthday or the Jewish woman or both have got him thinking about Jewishness in the context of continuity.

I don't know why or how, but suddenly I understood that by having a child with a Jewish woman, I would be part of a greater life, of a history, with a connection to generations that came before and would come after me. Maybe that's been the reason I never wanted to have a child before; I wasn't in the right culture. All my previous serious relationships have been with non-Jews. Seeing myself as a Jew, as having a Jewish mate, profoundly changed something in me, something that was less about just today and just me, and more about the relationship of the past to the present and to the future. Judaism suddenly became something of value to which I owed something of value: another generation.

I'm the last of the Kaluzny Jews. That's a responsibility, and it is powerful and scary.

While the motives for abandoning Judaism are varied, it is not difficult to follow the logic of Holocaust survivors. They paid a high price for their identity, and reasoned that if they disguised their heritage, they and their descendants would no longer be targeted for persecution.

What they did not necessarily factor into their decision was how difficult it is to keep so fundamental a secret. Nor did they anticipate their children's sense of entitlement, coupled with a lack of fear of prejudice. As Fern Levy told me, "I understand why my parents did what they did. I think they worried about our children and the possibility of discrimination, but I also feel deprived of not having a background in Judaism."

Children of Holocaust survivors who recapture the knowledge of their past do not necessarily embrace it, but neither are they cavalier. Their reactions vary from embarrassment to distress to relief to joy, but never blithe dismissal. The people I spoke to appraised the effect of their repressed or rejected history on their psyches, and weighed the ramifications. The serious consideration they gave the matter attests to its powerful centrality in the determination of identity.

Adoptees

I am a forty-three-year-old adoptee who just two and a half years ago found my birth mother after a search that went on and off for twenty-two years. I always wanted to know where I came from, what my heritage was, who I was. Yes, I love my adoptive parents and we have a good relationship. They even helped me in my search. But I wanted to know what everybody else knows . . . the basic facts of my identity.

When my son was born three years ago, he was the first person I ever laid eyes on who I was biologically related to. It was overwhelming to me . . . but it was strange. Why? I have dark brown hair and brown eyes. My husband has light brown hair and green eyes. My son has blue eyes! Where did that come from? When I took him for his first doctor's visit, I had to leave much of his medical history blank. I always hated that for me . . . but for him I hated it even more and I started searching again.

My husband does genealogy research. He knows his ancestors for generations. I know nothing. I asked him why he cares about his ancestors from three hundred years ago. He said it was interesting for many reasons, including knowing where he fits in history. I don't have that and I want it.

This posting to an adoption Internet Website speaks to the core issues of identity. Adoptees wrestle with the same demons as people who suddenly discovered Jewish ancestors. The basic questions of "Who am I?" and "Where did I come from?" and "Where do I fit in?" plague both. Before one person can relate to another, intimately or even superficially, he must know himself. He must have an internal touchstone, a base line by which to gauge the outside world.

The debate continues over whether we are biologically driven or environmentally molded. Are our tastes and inclinations genetically encoded? Of course, we are influenced by events, but how much of our basic makeup is charted by heredity? If nature supersedes nurture, then adoptees stand to gain a tremendous amount of self-knowledge by finding out about their birth parents.

The Minnesota Study of Twins Reared Apart begun in 1979 made a fascinating, though hardly conclusive, case for the effect of heredity on personality.[1] In that study, Thomas Bouchard and his co-authors found that separated twins exhibited the same taste in music, art, food, friends, careers, humor, athletics, hobbies, and so on. His findings were consistent even in cases where the twins were raised from birth in vastly different adoptive households. The study, though, has been criticized in some quarters for its narrow scope.

People who find out that they are of Jewish descent receive an information packet of tremendous import. They then have the task of assimilating that new information into their years-old image of self. Even to reject the information takes sizable psychic energy.

To be deprived of a personal history creates a mountainous challenge. It can leave an individual with a gnawing feeling of incompleteness. This disquiet is often inchoate. Many individuals told me that until they discovered their Jewish background, they felt a gap, an emptiness. They said they could not define it, but they knew something was missing. "I always felt incomplete. Nothing compares to knowing there's a piece out there not yet finalized."

Shelley was one of several adoptees in her family, but she was the only one who looked different. She had many unresolved emotional issues to work out, and as a result she became angry, unhappy, and disruptive. For one thing, she was raised in a religious household, but it was not a religion in which she found a spiritual home.

As long as I can remember, I knew I was adopted. I was raised in a very strong Latter Day Saints family. My adoptive grandmother is descended from Joseph Smith himself. I was the black sheep. Growing up, I experimented with drugs, sex, alcohol—which was all the more far out considering the family I was in.

I was always looking for some explanation of why I didn't fit in. I was so different: loud and with a wild streak a mile wide. I even look different. I have olive skin, dark hair, and dark eyes. Most of the neighborhood looks like the Aryan Nation. Everyone's blond and blue-eyed. Even my two adoptive brothers have fair skin and blue eyes. With my looks, I really stick out in family pictures.

I've always been interested in Middle Eastern studies, especially Hebrew. It's funny how fate works out. Eight years ago, when I registered at college, I had been considering chemistry, but I got to the campus a day late and missed chemistry orientation day. So I went the next day, which turned out to be Middle East studies orientation. I met the director of the program, who I found to be a pretty intriguing guy. I really wanted to study Hebrew, but everyone said to take Arabic, it's used in more countries, it'll be more useful.

Shelley had been struggling with her Mormon identity. She found she could not relate to the tenets of the faith. Coming from a religious family, community, and university, she found her inability to relate confusing. Just about that time, friends told her about Brigham Young University's Jerusalem Center on Mount Scopus. Her friends had studied Old and New Testament history there, which particularly interested Shelley. Best of all, everyone came back spouting glowing testimonials. In what was to be a life-altering decision, Shelley decided to sign up for the Israel program.

There was one particular teacher in Jerusalem I really grew to respect and appreciate. Because of what he taught us about Jewish history and culture, he opened me up to wanting to know more about Judaism. He even took kids to his home to show them the holidays firsthand.

After a while I started feeling an affinity. And people thought I belonged there too. In Tel Aviv, I was strolling with a large group of students from school, mostly fair-skinned, blue-eyed kids, and this older couple came over to me, asking me questions in Hebrew. This happened a lot. Apparently, I looked like I fit in with the landscape. I certainly had the right hair and skin color.

By the time I had been in Israel six months, I started to question more deeply where my identity lay, where I felt most connected. Before that, I had some curiosity, and did some minor digging for my biological family, but nothing serious.

Shelley came back from Israel determined to find her roots. With the help of her adoptive family, she hired a professional adoption finder, who located her birth mother, now a faithful Mormon, living in Idaho. Shelley got to know her, visited her family. She even discovered some half-brothers. Shelley's mother wanted her to learn about the family so they talked and looked at photos.

In high school, her mother had had a best friend, a Latter Day Saints member. When that friend went to Utah for college, Shelley's mother followed her. On the heels of an unsuccessful love affair, she got pregnant on the rebound by her ex-boyfriend's roommate. At nineteen, she didn't feel she could be a good mother, and the father wasn't interested in raising an infant, so she consulted with a trusted professor, who directed her to Latter Day Saints social services. Shelley was placed at three days old.

My biological mother was raised Catholic but had a lot of contact with the Jewish community in Minneapolis. Those were her friends, for whatever reason. Her father's last name was White and her mother's maiden name was Margaret Flaum. Her mother's mother was Stern. They were German. My mother always thought her mother was Catholic. With a name like Margaret, she certainly sounded Catholic. I got the impression my mother didn't know the family history very well. Looking through family photos, I found a picture of my grandmother, Margaret. She was very beautiful. In a stereotypical way, she looks Jewish. I even commented to my mother, "Gee, Grandma Maggie looks really Jewish."

That was in October. The following February, I went to Minneapolis to meet Grandma Maggie. She showed me more family pictures. We found Great-grandmother Stern's photo. My mom offhandedly remarked, "Shelley thinks we look Jewish." Grandma said, "Well, we are. We're a bunch of German Jews!" My mother's jaw dropped. "Yeah," Grandma said, "we used to be Jewish. Now we're Catholic. It's part of the past. So be it. It's no big deal."

My ears perked up. I was Jewish . . . all the pieces clicked together all of a sudden, like "k'ting!" Everything made sense. I can't even say exactly what it explained but it did. It felt like a kind of completion.

Shelley decided to learn more. Back at the University of Utah, she enrolled in Jewish history and Israeli culture classes. She met a Jewish boy from Baltimore in Arabic class, and peppered him with questions. He offered to put her in touch with his rabbi and she eagerly accepted.

The rabbi said, "Normally I'd tell you, there's no need for you to be a Jew; just be a good Mormon. But since you probably are Jewish by birth, I advise you to study for conversion, especially since you don't have conclusive genealogy records."

I'd never had a lot of exposure to Judaism. In Utah there's a small Jewish population—one Lubavitch Hasidic community center in Salt Lake and a Reform/Conservative synagogue. I dated a few of the Jewish guys around, but even so, I had such a limited understanding and knowledge of what Judaism was, other than the fact that it was somehow different from what I was raised with. I knew Chanukah and Passover and the kosher laws from grade school because I was friends with a Jewish boy in my class.

Shelley took the rabbi's advice and enrolled in an introduction to Judaism class at a local Utah synagogue. She made a few trips back to the rabbi in Baltimore to study, and in September 1995, he officiated at her conversion. Shelley was given the Hebrew name Sarah, after the first female Jew (the first female convert to Judaism, in a sense). He added a middle name, Tsiona, to reflect Shelley's love of Zion.

Knowing that Judaism does not solicit converts, and in fact discourages them, Shelley expected an intense grilling from the rabbinical court, but her rabbi had apparently explained her family background to them. They asked if she understood the burden she was assuming, and whether she was willing to observe Jewish law and raise her future children as Jews. She agreed, then dunked in the ritual bath. The three rabbis stood behind the door so they could hear her recite the blessings.

Even though I knew they weren't watching, I felt bad about my ankle tattoo. I had it put on way before I knew I was Jewish, before I knew tattoos are forbidden for Jews. It's a tattoo of the Hebrew word, "chai," the good luck word for long life.

I don't live near enough to a synagogue to walk to services on the Sabbath. I haven't koshered the kitchen either. I get some flack from the local rabbi for that, but I live with my parents, so it's really their kitchen. I do the best I can. I eat vegetarian. I celebrate Passover with friends. I'll probably end up on the East Coast, where I'm applying to med school.

I'm close with the Israelis here. Some of my professor friends are Israeli. For me, it's an identity thing. It's more cultural than religious.

Shelley felt from her youngest days that she was different from the rest of her adoptive family. For one thing, she looked different. But for another, she did not share their spiritual leanings. Even though they were adopted, her siblings embraced the Mormon faith. It was not until she found her birth mother and her birth religion that Shelley attained a feeling of completion and self-recognition.

There is a tremendous poignancy to the situation of the adoptee. No matter how early in life the adoption transpires, the adopted child must grapple with the fact that she was born to one parent but raised by another. As often as the child may be reassured that her birth mother gave her up because she loved her, because she wanted the best for her, the reality that she relinquished her parental role flies in the face of any protestations of love. The adoptee may be placed in a loving, nurturing home, and may be assured daily that it was for noble reasons that her parent(s) placed her for adoption, but at some point, the adoptee must struggle with those paradoxical ideas, integrate them, and come to terms with them. This is part of identity formation.

It is hard to ignore the irony in the name James Longing. James is a forty-year-old man whose life, at least from his perspective, was characterized by rejection. As heartbreaking as his childhood was, though, his story has a happy ending, or at least a sense of positive closure.

I have known I was adopted since I was young. That fact had a huge effect on my outlook on life. I call it retinal. It shapes the window through which I see everything. It becomes part of the window itself.

I often wonder whether adoptive children know preconsciously that they were adopted. Do they know they were rejected by their mother, which is how adoptees see it? I think so. I think there is an intuition at work, some kind of bond that formed over the nine months in the womb.

My adoptive father, John Raymond Longing, is from a pre-Revolutionary War family. His family members were college-educated, church-going Christians. My mother's parents came from Armenia. She grew up in Brooklyn. Her father was a hard-working, driven, intelligent man. In her day, Brooklyn was a tough immigrant scene. She had a brilliant sister she could never compete with, so she grew up feeling stupid and inferior. It was a cold, distant household, and she treated us the same way she was raised. (My siblings are all adopted. One sister is a Pueblo Indian.)

I suspect she saw the Jewish immigrants in her neighborhood as some kind of model. She's certainly not anti-Semitic. I heard from an early age that Jews are a special people. She said they were incredibly productive, accomplished people, that they're disproportionately represented in literature, science, art, every field of endeavor. She used to tell me, we feel you have a Jewish mind. I took that to mean a good mind.

When I turned eighteen, my mother told me in an offhanded way that my biological mother was Jewish. As soon as I heard that, I started telling people I was Jewish. Because I'm fair-haired, fair-skinned, and blue-eyed, people didn't believe me, but it turns out I look more like my biological mother than her other five kids do. My girlfriend's mother refused to believe I was Jewish because she said no Jewish mother would ever give up her child. So all in all, I grew up with an adoptive mother who kept me at arm's length, and I was the son of a woman who rejected me at birth.

Finding out I was Jewish seemed right. It's not that I intuited it, but it fit in with my psychology of rejection. I felt rejected, and the Jews were a rejected people. A perfect fit!

Every few years I tried to find my mother. Then, when I was twenty-nine, my adoptive mother gave me the court order of adoption. I used property records to track her down. Then I went to the registrar of marriages and found her married name. I looked her husband up in a telephone book and wrote her a letter. Five days later, I called. A girl answered. "She's at work." She gave me the work number, and I reached her. As soon as I said my name, I heard her say, "I saw the envelope on my desk and I knew without opening it. I knew it was the letter I'd been waiting for for years." She had even registered with adoption services in order to be found more easily.

She was from a family of Austrian Jews who came to the States at the end of the nineteenth century. Her parents were divorced and she moved to the West Coast with her mother and her sister. When she was eighteen, she had a one-night fling with a twenty-year-old Marine. I haven't tried to find him. She left town to have an "operation" and gave me to a private adoption agency.

Since finding her, we've become very close. We're deeply, utterly reunited. Her husband's a great guy. He knows all about me. I went to Israel with her for a week so I could meet her son, my half-brother. I also have a cousin there. I've met her sister and I knew her mother, my grandmother, for a brief time.

Even though I'm circumcised, I feel I can only technically claim to be Jewish. After all, I was an altar boy for five years. I love Mass. I'm married to an Eastern Orthodox woman who was born in Yugoslavia. She came here in the sixties. She's pro-Palestinian, so there's some tension on that issue. In fact, she's from a faintly anti-Semitic family. We have two sons, Aaron and Lavi. We don't raise them with any religion, but they were baptized into the Serbian Orthodox Church, which was important to my in-laws. My older son is seven. He knows I have two mothers. We see Savta (we call my biological mother by the Hebrew word for grandma) more than we see my adoptive mother.

I can't feel comfortable saying I'm Jewish. Being Jewish has a definite meaning, none of which really attaches to me. I have become irrationally pro-Israel, though. I never had anything to believe in before Israel. It's the cause I've always wanted.

Psychiatrists David Brodzinsky and Marshall Schechter specialize in treating and researching adoption issues. They suggest that adoptees who search for their birth parents are seeking completion.[2] They do not necessarily need to "start over," they simply need to resolve where they came from and who they are.

It may be that reactions to this kind of stressful discovery can vary according to a person's sense of control. Someone who feels tossed around by external events, vulnerable to circumstances, is likely to feel ineffectual when it comes to taking command of his own direction. Conversely, someone who believes that determination and strength of will can make changes is likely to invest energy in making those changes.

People who feel more in control are less likely to be stressed and buffeted by the surprises life throws their way. Some will welcome the new information, explore it, try it on for size. Some will deny their sense of displacement or minimize the importance of the discovery. In response to finding out they or their ancestors are Jewish, they might well respond, "That's nice, dear."

Such a one is Peggy Alstrom, a writer and editor in her mid-thirties, who saw my query on the Internet. Her response was breezy and self-assured. Peggy found out through a genealogical search that she is of Jewish descent, but her sense of self was already so fully formed that she regarded her discovery as peripheral, or, as she calls it, a "non-issue."

I was adopted (and raised) by my grandparents, who, as far as I know, may have had no knowledge of having Jewish ancestors. My grandfather was Swedish, while my grandmother had invented a remarkable fantasy story of being descended from British aristocracy. Of all the things my mother and aunt were told about "the family background," virtually nothing on their mother's side was true.

By the time my grandmother died, most of the surviving family was aware that her stories were false, and my biological aunt (my adoptive sister) hired a genealogist to begin searching for "the real story." Eventually we tracked down a descendant of grandmother's sister, a man who had also compiled extensive genealogical research on his family.

We found out that Grandmother's ancestors were Idaho farmers. She grew up first in Idaho and then in Southern California. Grandfather was raised in San Francisco, also from a farming background.

We have speculated since her death that some sort of rift occurred within her own family. We know now that her parents separated some years after she was born, and her own birth apparently caused some sort of trouble in the family. She had told us that her parents died in the 1920s; we subsequently learned that her father had been alive, in fact, until the late 1950s—but no one in the family ever knew of his existence or of the existence of other relatives who were also living at the time. We were, in a sense, cut off, adrift from any sense of "roots."

The genealogical search showed up some Jewish ancestry in the late 1870s, when Pamela Kezia Flaxbaum married Jacob Cartwright Jamison. It is difficult to tell whether Jacob's ancestry is Jewish; the names are fairly Anglo, with an occasional Sarah or David or Eli. Jewish names crop up throughout all branches of the family tree: Mordecai, Jeremiah, et cetera.

If my grandmother was aware of Jewish ancestry, she never mentioned it to anyone in her family, and I would not be surprised if she was, in fact, unaware of it herself. I have no idea what caused the rift in her family, but I doubt it had anything to do with Judaism. Though my grandmother claimed to be Episcopal in background, she was not a religious person throughout most of her life. In her final years, she expressed an interest in returning to church, and appeared quite familiar with all the rituals of the Episcopal service.

Thus, to put it in a nutshell, the discovery of our "Jewish background" was a complete non-issue in our family. We were unaware of it until genealogical research uncovered the names of ancestors from the 1800s. By this time, my sister had entered the Episcopal Church herself, because she was the one who had to take Grandmother there. And I had become a born-again Christian. My sister/aunt and I did not feel that this had anything significant to do with us, or who we are now. We both regard our heritage as "interesting," but not as being in any way defining of who we are today. In earlier years, I'd never felt particularly strongly one way or another. I hold a strong respect for Judaism based on my Christian beliefs, but certainly have no interest in embracing either Judaism or Islam. My belief is based upon the content of the faith, rather than on the genes within my bloodstream.

Robert Taft, having discovered that his father's mother was Jewish, expressed dismay at not being universally accepted as a Jew. Robert thinks of himself as part-Jewish. He has no cultural markers when it comes to Jewishness, but because of his ancestry he identifies ethnically as Irish-Jewish. His religion, Catholicism, is a separate matter entirely.

I was adopted at the age of three and a half by a devout Anglican couple, very conservative in their outlook. They told my adopted sister and me that we were adopted almost as soon as we could understand the term. They changed my name from David to Robert. They wanted to make a clean break. I wish they had kept my given name. It would have given me a sense of continuity. You can't make a clean break with the past, can you. (Well, perhaps you can. You can run to another country, change your name, et cetera. But this reduces your humanity.)

At age eighteen, I converted to Catholicism, which caused them considerable pain. For one thing, Catholicism struck me as the only logical form of Christianity. I was entranced by Scholastic theology in the form of St. Thomas Aquinas. (I am sure that, had things been a bit different, I could well have become an enthusiastic rabbinical scholar!) And Catholicism has a call to holiness that appeals to me. (I would add that I like Hasidism for similar reasons.) And to be perfectly honest, now that I'm older, I can see that my conversion was a form of teenage rebellion.

In my late thirties, I came across the address of someone who assists adoptees in locating their natural families. I contacted him and we found my biological mother, who told me the family history. My parents had met at a Communist Party dance. Their relationship was not happy and broke down within two years after I was born. I was their only child. My father's mother was from a well-off Jewish family in London. The family name was Hirst, an anglicized form of Hertz. The family had become Christian by my grandmother's time. She and my father had died by the time I traced them, but I met his two subsequent children, my half-brother and half-sister. To my disappointment, my half-siblings are not very interested in the Jewish dimension of our background.

When I found out about my Jewish grandmother, I was very pleased, but a bit disappointed that she was on my father's side, and so doesn't count for halakhic [Jewish legal] purposes.

I had been mildly interested in Judaism before this, and had undertaken an introductory course in Hebrew shortly before finding out my family background. Since then, I have maintained a low-key but continuing interest in Judaism. I subscribed to an email Talmud class for a while, but I had to drop it for lack of time. On a lighter note, I have developed a good repertoire of Jewish jokes, which I tell at the slightest provocation. This, combined with my genealogy, has led my friends to address me as "Rabbi."

Learning about my Jewish ancestry has intensified my attitude to Judaism. I was always sympathetic towards it, but I have the feeling that it is such a closed world that it's not possible to identify with it. Perhaps a reasonably accessible route is to read novels, which give a surrogate growing up experience. I recently read Rabbis and Wives *by Chaim Grade. Beautiful stories about turn of the century Jews in Lithuania. And Chaim Potok is one of my favorites.*

I guess the Holocaust and Israel are the points of entry for newcomers. I've always been sensitive to the Holocaust. For one thing, it's been getting increasing coverage in the media through books and movies like Schindler's List. *I don't think, though, that I have an adequate appreciation of the enormity of evil manifested in the Nazi regime. If I knew of relatives who had perished in the Holocaust, I bet I would be more alive to the horror of it.*

On the question of Israel, I was brought up as a political conservative, so we were always pro-Israel. I am still emotionally pro-Israel, but have become troubled at what seem to me systematic injustices to the Palestinian Arabs. I've been there once, and spent the whole time hanging around Jerusalem. Some people are turned off by the complexity of it all, but I loved it. The history of the city is so much more explicit than in, say, London or Paris. And I loved the diversity of the people.

The discovery of my Jewish roots has come too late to be significant in my personality formation. Religiously, I remain a committed Catholic, increasingly aware and positive about the Church's Jewish roots. But for a recent questionnaire that asked for ethnic background, I put down "Irish-Jewish."

Robert was self-aware enough to realize that his conversion to Catholicism was partly motivated by anger. He did, after all, experience several painful disruptions. Three and a half years old is a developmentally vulnerable age at which to be transplanted into a new family. And to be christened with a new name sends a clear message of a break with the past. He had to have been very flexible and emotionally resourceful to deal with so much fundamental change.

Whereas Robert went looking for his parents, Janie Miller, a Jewish woman, sought no one. Her Palestinian father came looking for her. He dropped into his daughter's life when she was twenty-nine, and dropped back out not long after, making a profound impression on her in that interim period of reunion. Israel figured prominently in the wake of his departure, a wake comprised of waves of dissension and confusion.

Janie always knew she and her brother were adopted. She is five foot two and dark; her brother is a foot taller and blond. He used to joke with her, "Don't walk down the street with me. People will think you're my girlfriend, not my sister." The couple who adopted Janie are Conservative Jews. Janie went to Hebrew school and had a bat mitzvah ceremony.

When Janie was twenty, she went to live in Belgium for her junior year abroad. The college program required medical approval. She could have gotten a checkup and sent the doctor's report, but she decided to write to the adoption agency for her medical history. They sent a summary of her background, telling her that both her parents were college graduates and that her mother had had a difficult pregnancy.

Nine years ago I got a phone call from the agency saying my birth father, Michael, wanted to know if I would like to meet him and my birth mother. Michael married a German woman and had a child with her soon after my birth, but he and my birth mother stayed in touch over the years. In order to meet them, I had to go to probate court and fill out papers, and my birth mother had to write a letter saying it was okay with her, which Michael convinced her to do. She was reluctant, not knowing if I had been affected by her sickness during pregnancy.

I asked my adoptive parents about it. My father had suffered many losses in his life, including an uncle in World War II. This was threatening to him. He was afraid of losing me, but the probate judge is his fishing buddy and reassured him.

I stipulated that we only correspond at first. Michael didn't like that so much, but we did it. Then in October I called Diane, my birth mother, then Michael. He told me that there had been a lightning storm near his house during which he had an epiphany that made it clear he needed to find me.

We decided to meet for lunch. It was a rainy day. They showed me photos. I have my father's bushy eyebrows and my mother's lithe body. They met in college when she was nineteen and he was twenty. They fell in love, or lust. I was born a year later and placed for adoption at six weeks. They both had an inkling I'd been placed with a Jewish family because the agency asked my mother for permission to do so.

Anything I know about them is from what I've been told. I don't know how much is true. They were from very different cultural backgrounds. She was from a working-class American family; he is Palestinian-American. His father is from the West Bank, and his mother is Syrian. Diane re-

members her family remarking how dark Michael was. I'm olive-skinned, but not very dark.

My immediate reaction was, who are these people in my universe? Are they family? Friends? Future friends? Will they be the answer to all my questions? What will I mean to them?

Diane's children were shocked to find out about my existence. I was close with them for a while, and with Michael's son. Michael was very anti-Israel. That played out a bit between us. We lost touch because he stopped calling me. I wasn't what he expected and his enthusiasm waned.

Ever since Michael questioned things I said about Israel, I've done some reading and developed close Palestinian women friends. Activists. That's been a source of difficulty with my adoptive father. My parents avoid talking about it with me. My stepmother sometimes says, "Those pro-Palestinian people." And she can stop a conversation cold with a remark about Golda Meir saying Israeli boys didn't know how to shoot until Arab boys forced them to.

When I visited my parents in Florida, they had a newspaper clipping on the fridge with the headline, "Israel's mere existence a thorn in the side of Palestinians." I don't think they put it up just because I was coming, but I felt it was about me anyway. We can't discuss it anymore. They went on a trip to Israel last fall with the Jewish Federation. Before they left I wrote them a letter saying I hoped they would tour Israel with open eyes even though it was a pro-Israel sponsored trip. But they shut their eyes anyway. Dad says I've been brainwashed. I said, even though I know the Palestinian experience isn't comparable to the Holocaust, still, the early events of the Holocaust are similar to what's going on there now. On Passover I bring readings about freedom and human rights to the Seder table.

Last week I went to a talk on the thirtieth anniversary of the Palestinian Occupation. The speaker was Jewish and very critical of Israel. On the other hand, I can't speak up during an anti-Arab conversation and say, hey, you're talking about ME.

I've had to reassess a lot. I haven't found a Jewish community that I'm comfortable in. It would have to be a very open one. I go back and forth.

Ever since the State of Israel was established, nationality has figured into the definition of Jewish identity. According to its constitution,

Israel is a Jewish state. The Law of Return, which stipulates that a Jew who moves to Israel may become a citizen, intertwines the two, nationality and identity, even more. So when Janie talks about the complexity created in her life when she absorbed her Palestinian father's views, she is touching on a very complicated turn of events.

Twenty-six-year-old Hana Mehdi, a graduate student in literature and film studies in the Midwest, experienced the opposite situation. She grew up thinking she was the daughter of an Irish-American mother and a Syrian-Palestinian father. Just three months before she saw my author's query, Hana learned that a Jewish man had fathered her.

All my life people have been telling me I look Jewish. My mother is from a working-class Irish family. They're very conservative, racist really. The military sent them to Texas, and that's where my mother went to college and met the man I always thought was my father. He came to the States from Lebanon at age six. His undergraduate degree is from the American University in Beirut, and his Ph.D. is from the University of Texas.

The day after they got married, he told her he was infertile. He had participated in a medical study and learned that he had a low sperm count, which he thought meant no *sperm count. She was livid. She felt tricked and left him. He had the marriage annulled. Meanwhile, she went back to El Paso and lived in an abandoned church in a hippie community. She fell in love with a photographer there, David. They had a passionate relationship, even though she knew he was engaged to a Jewish woman in Denmark. Even when she became pregnant, it was understood that he was not going to break his engagement. When the time came, he went to Denmark as planned, married, and had a daughter. He took the money his parents had given him as a wedding gift and gave it to my mother for an abortion, but she used it to buy a tent and went to live in the Mojave Desert.*

My Palestinian father kept in touch with my mother's parents. He was worried about her, and came back to find her. He decided that for all intents and purposes I would be his daughter and raised me to believe I was his own beloved child. After I was born, they had a boy and a girl together, but recently decided to divorce.

My mother went back to El Paso, to take care of her dying mother. One day, on a whim, she looked David up in the phone book. He had come back to New York from Denmark, got involved with drugs, and moved to El Paso to dry out. He knew my mother had not had the abortion and had taken up again with my father. He thought I had grown up in the Middle East with my mother and her husband. He pretty much forgot about me and figured we'd meet one day on opposite sides of a battlefield in the Persian Gulf.

When I got engaged, my mother figured it was time for me to know my true history. She drank way too much one night and told me the story, complete with photographs. David had done a photo documentary on a brothel, and she showed me pictures of him sitting on the lap of a prostitute with a can of beer in his hand. My Arab father is so different, so proper.

I think she did it to get back at my dad because of the divorce. He's very afraid our relationship is threatened by David's reappearance. He calls a lot. She didn't tell me about him very well. I wish my parents had sat me down and said, this is the story, and we love you. My mother is not a stupid woman. She's a social worker with a couple of graduate degrees.

I'm angry, but I don't like being angry. I'm finding out that parents aren't superheroes. This was a stunning moment in that sense. They've been lying to me all these years.

I met David, my father, a month ago. We've been in touch on email and on the phone. We didn't talk about Judaism, but I know his parents were very religious. They kept kosher and went to temple every week. His father died, but he told his mother about me. She's disappointed that my mother's not Jewish.

My future mother-in-law, on the other hand, is thrilled that I have a Jewish father. She's Sephardic but very secularized. I've been to temple more than my fiancé has. I was shocked to find out their family eats pork.

I don't have to rethink my stance. It posed a problem for David. He thought I would hate him because he's Jewish. That was painful to me. When you grow up Arab, you're constantly faced with people who think you're automatically anti-Jewish. I still haven't had to face being asked, what are you? I don't know what I'll say. I think I'll say I'm Arab-Jewish-Irish.

I have a lot of Jewish friends at the university. They used to tease me that I'm not really Arab. Give it up, Hana, they used to say. Tell us you're interracial. Now I'm thinking, Shit! They were right!

The interviewees included in this chapter experienced tumultuous assaults on their identity. They had to resolve their feelings about being adopted, and integrate their knowledge of their biological parentage with that of their adoptive family. The instances related in this chapter reflect the different definitions of what it means to be Jewish: ethnic, cultural, religious, political.

James latched on to Israel as his tether to Judaism. Peggy, respectful of all creeds, made an intellectual choice to adopt Christianity based on its theological tenets. Janie and Hana have to come to terms with an entirely different aspect of Jewishness, the geopolitical aspect as represented by the Israeli-Palestinian conflict. Each was committed to a position and then found in her genealogy a challenge of sorts. And Robert sounds wistful but open to learning about Jewish culture without actually being Jewish. Having given the matter much thought, his conclusion is that Judaism takes root more easily when it has been practiced within a family context. As he commented, "It's very complicated and hard to get into. Perhaps because it's so family-based, it's exceptionally difficult to absorb if you don't marry into it."

Robert observed that Judaism is very behavioral. It is characterized by numerous prescriptions and proscriptions. Unlike the individual whose memories, for example, of a Passover Seder table laden with traditional foods, of customs, and of the participation of extended family provide a positive Jewish model and memory bank, the newcomer to Judaism is presented with a formidable body of knowledge, history, and practice. More important, perhaps, the Jew-from-birth also has a familiarity with the rituals that reduces their foreign and overwhelming nature. People who come late to Judaism are confronted by an intimidating game of catch-up. It takes a profound drive to convert to Judaism. The convert joins a community that has a painful history and an endless array of responsibilities.

Clearly for Shelley, the youngest, the discovery that her maternal grandmother was Jewish served as a catalyst for change. She welcomed the news as a validation of her choice and a confirmation that she was continuing a bloodline. For an adoptee, that was a deeply meaningful discovery.

Conclusions

Paul Goldreich is a London psychoanalyst whose practice is heavily comprised of Holocaust survivors, among whom are numerous patients with reclaimed identities, identities they had to struggle to remember. He has worked with several people who were between the ages of six months and a year when they were placed in hiding at the beginning of the war, and grew up Catholic or Protestant. They always had a feeling of being different, he said, especially the women.

Goldreich observed that "the re-emergence into Jewish life is a slow, torturous process. And not everyone returns—there are also people who were hidden in Christian settings, usually at a slightly older age, who refused to go back to Judaism." His observation reminded me of Stefanie (Stefa) Seltzer who, together with her Jewish husband, raised her children as Jews but lost her own faith in God. Stefanie, today a resident of Philadelphia, was smuggled out of the Polish Radomsko ghetto at age three and a half. She was shuffled from home to home, seven settings altogether, answering to different names in different places. Some took her in for money, others out of compassion. At different points, her mother was able to join her for a while. Her prescient mother even hired someone to teach Stefa to pray as a Catholic.

After the war, we stayed in Poland a few months. People came to my mother and said, "It's Passover. The Jews need the blood of Christian children to bake their matzo. Be sure you don't let Stefa out by herself." I knew she was worried after this conversation, and I continued to kneel in prayer. I wanted her to be comfortable, so I pretended to be Catholic even though by this time I knew we were Jewish. My mother was not a believer. Deep down, yes, when she was sick she turned to God. I tried to believe when I was sixteen, but I couldn't be convinced.

Today I am not observant but my children are. I raised my children never telling them I didn't believe. I just never spoke about God. I always said, "This is what we do," not, "This is what we believe." I believe in ethics and in man's relationship to man. The important thing is to be a decent human being.

Stefa is a social worker and speaks frequently at Holocaust gatherings. She founded Champions of Caring, a project that honors high school students who do good deeds in the community, and cofounded the Federation of Jewish Child Survivors of the Holocaust, comprised of thirty-nine chapters worldwide.

Goldreich said that a high percentage of hidden children and children of survivors become psychologists and psychotherapists—something I found to be true among all the people I interviewed, not just these populations. "There is a reparative aspect to their career choice. They are repairing the world and themselves."

Then he said, "To my mind, the most important question is, how does someone get reconnected, consciously or unconsciously, with their Jewishness? It seems to me, child survivors have a reservoir of memory. That's how I have come to know it. They just need little instances to remind them. Something triggers the reservoir to react."

I related to Goldreich an anecdote Blair Crosby had shared: "When I first started spending time with my husband, we went in the summer to visit his Jewish grandfather in Far Rockaway. In those days, it was a bungalow colony. His grandfather spoke to me in Yiddish and I understood everything he said! He got a kick out of it, and I couldn't explain how I did it!"

Goldreich's explanation was that Blair had probably overheard her parents speaking Yiddish when she was quite young, and retained enough of it to understand what she was hearing. The same thing happened to Jewish convert Gabrielle Glaser, author of *Strangers to the Tribe: Portraits of Interfaith Marriage.*[1] In her book about Jewish-Gentile couples, Glaser mentions that the more she looked into her Lutheran great-grandparents' history, the more convinced she became that they were German Jews.

Two years after her book was published, a first cousin to Glaser's father contacted her after hearing her speak on National Public Radio, and provided details that make Glaser certain her suspicions were correct. She was shown photographs of her great-grandfather in typically Jewish garb. And like Blair, Glaser attended a Jewish funeral where she found herself mouthing the words to a Hebrew prayer along with the assemblage. A psychologist friend of hers suggested that she must have intuited clues to her background as she was growing up, clues her father may not have even known he was giving.

Was this, then, the explanation for why Yossi in "Children of Survivors" felt compelled to take actions that would change his entire life when he read a headline about war in Israel? Was it intuition that propelled this young man to take an Abrahamic journey from his birthplace in Holland to his new home in Israel?

Goldreich was certain that Yossi's mother retained certain behaviors particular to Jews, and that Yossi could not help but make inferences. "Parents who deny their Jewishness nevertheless inevitably send out signals. They leave clues that their children pick up on, though neither side—parent or child—may be consciously aware of what is happening." His earlier use of the term "reservoir of memory" rang familiar to me, and when I returned home, I scoured my collection of hidden child newsletters. There, in an essay by Canadian psychiatrist (and hidden child) Robert Krell, I found that he, too, talked about "a floodgate of memory that needed to be released or it would devour us."[2] I solicited his reaction to Goldreich's theory, and to a large extent he concurred. "I think it's hard for parents not to, from time to time, give a hint. There may be a thousand slips of the tongue which the child does not connect to being Jewish. Yet there is a subtle awareness. The question becomes: when does the observation get crystallized by the child into the construct, 'Perhaps I am a Jew?'"

That had been Yaakov Nakache's reaction (see the "Prologue") when the possibility arose ever so tangentially that he might be Jewish. Yaakov could certainly have converted to Catholicism and proceeded with his plans for the priesthood. He was at the top of his class, spiritual, devoted. Why reject all that just because his mother's parents were assimilated Jews?

"I always ask," says Goldreich, "why do these people, who were raised as non-Jews, come here to the Holocaust Survivors' Center? Why don't they go to a private psychologist or psychiatrist? Why go to a

Jewish agency? And the answer is, because this is home. Here he can be who he is. With his parents, who are in denial, he can't be himself. Once you can identify with your feelings, you are integrated. You match up the internal and the external to reach a consistent identity, inside and out." In clinical terms, Goldreich is referring to the concept of cognitive dissonance, wherein a person's beliefs are at odds with his experience, causing emotional unrest. As defined by psychologist Leon Festinger, cognitive dissonance arises because people crave harmony, and so they will find a way to make an adjustment in a conflicting belief or behavior in order to eliminate, or at least minimize, any disharmony.[3]

Krell alludes to cognitive dissonance when he discusses the current generation of East Europeans who are learning for the first time that they are descended from Jews who perished in World War II.

> When they're the recipients of a deathbed confession from their foster parents, as in Poland, that they're Jewish, they immediately feel comfortable because they always knew they were different. I don't know if they're feeling a comfort with Judaism or just relief at knowing why they have felt different. They were probably always suspecting. After all, there are physical differences, as when a child is dark and curly-haired and the rest of the family is blond and straight-haired. Maybe they overheard whispers, "She is starting to look Jewish," et cetera. I was a hidden child in Holland. I can tell you from personal experience that everything around you sends signals. Everyone colludes in the secret, even the neighbors.

Anyone who did not always know his true history, including hidden children, could suffer from cognitive dissonance. Historian Yael Zerubavel points to the Christian conversion narratives, which can contain a similarity between a sudden revelation of hidden identity and the experience of conversion. In both one may feel the need to reorganize one's biography. Anselm Strauss, talking about feelings of discontinuity, assures us that "past identities can be reconciled, made to appear uniform despite their apparent diversity, only if they can be encompassed in a unified interpretation . . . Thus, a late convert to a sect may view most of his life as actually spent in the service of the Lord and regard the early wastrel years as a necessary preparation to the later service."[4]

Offering two explanations for this phenomenon, Zerubavel suggested, first, that people might reorganize their conscious memories in order to confirm their new information. The conversion may create a desire to identify the buried roots of one's new identity in the old, pre-conversion past in order to highlight a hidden continuity. A person who finds out she is Jewish might revisit her memories of Jewish friends or books on Jewish subjects that she particularly enjoyed. These memories would then foster a sense of having been drawn to Judaism.

Second, Zerubavel explained that unconscious memories float to the surface when new information helps release them. Repressed memories are unleashed when one remembers a suppressed past. This frequently happens when one experiences an invasion of one's self or a sense of rupture with one's identity. Mental health professionals often use reconstructive therapy to loosen their patients' repressive grip on unpleasant memories. For example, if a Holocaust survivor were to present with amnesia, the therapist might show the patient photographs of home or ask questions about childhood festive meals or foods, probing nonthreatening areas that would ease the patient into remembering more and more about the pretraumatic past in the safety of the doctor's office. Slowly the patient retrieves suppressed memories and weaves them into her consciousness. Once the patient gets in touch with her pre-Holocaust identity, she is able to integrate that former life with the present and become whole, or at least start on the road to recovery.

This "reservoir of memory" theory left me wondering about Jewish infants adopted at birth by non-Jews (or vice-versa), who express that same homecoming feeling when they uncovered their biological roots. Did they fall into the category of resolving cognitive dissonance? Maybe—having been told they were adopted, or looking different from the rest of the family, or having happened upon documents or rumors—they experienced the relief of finding out a truth about their background. Or was there another explanation?

The concept of the immortal Jewish soul has scant support in mainstream textual sources. Rabbi Lawrence Epstein recalls a Talmudic comment on a verse in Deuteronomy (29:14) which indicates that all Jewish souls, past, present, and future, were present at the revelation on Mount Sinai. The Talmud in Tractate Sabbath interprets this verse to include converts, whose spirits were in attendance as well, implying that converts have Jewish souls that got misdirected into non-Jewish bodies, and returned to their destiny upon conversion.

This view is reminiscent of Jung's theory of the collective unconscious: "the contents of the collective unconscious have never been individually acquired, but owe their existence exclusively to heredity."[5] An individual's unconscious is comprised of forgotten or suppressed thoughts, memories, and experiences, but there exist shared cultural forms, archetypes, which are passed on generation to generation as the same collective unconscious. Was the Talmud saying the revelation at Sinai was a group-specific collective unconscious memory? An interesting thought.

Never having been empirically proven, the concept of the collective unconscious is highly arguable. Yet those very words, "collective unconscious," were offered by way of explanation from several of the people I interviewed who were speaking from their own instincts.

Hi, Barbara.

Today the second person called to tell me about your ad in the Book Review. It is interesting to me that your interest in this subject comes out of curiosity . . . Mine comes through living a life of outwardly fitting in and inwardly feeling a lack of belonging. My Jewish identity was confirmed at age sixteen by an aunt. My father was livid. Both my late parents were Jewish. My father came here at age sixteen from Rumania. He decided he wasn't a Jew because he considered Judaism a religion, not a race, and he didn't believe in Judaism. My mother went along. There were visits over the years by family members who were Jewish but I was taught not to notice the differences. It was confusing for me. Years later I realized I felt cheated, ripped off and betrayed. I feel like I had a right to know. There was confusion, secrets, issues of identity, begging to be heard and understood, wanting to figure out who I really was. I became a psychotherapist interested, of course, in identity issues.

Have you found any interesting patterns thus far? I'm interested in what you are discovering. I had a lot of shame and fear around being Jewish. I love it discovering that some have so much pride in being Jewish. I've been doing a lot of exploring. I love going to hear Hebrew chanting. It resonates in me. I think it's in the genes, the collective unconscious. I'd be surprised if that weren't true. Even though I don't know if I subscribe to the theology, I'm Jewish. I'm studying but I don't think it will ever be something I feel is mine. But I'm a Jew. I feel more complete now that in the past few years I seem to have broken through some major block about owning my own Jewishness. As if a hole was filled. My creativity was also more fully released and at last I feel that I am fully me.

Sincerely, Sally

Hi, Barbara.

My father never told my mother he was Jewish. He never mentioned any family or said he had none, which my mother had no reason to doubt until one day, while she was at our cottage and he was at work, two Jewish-looking men arrived in a car and announced they were his brothers. That was the first hint my mother had that he was Jewish. I knew it was not something to speak about. My mother raised me as an Episcopalian, which I didn't question but didn't internalize either. It seemed more of a carapace than a spine.

Several years ago, as the first female district manager at my newspaper, I was collecting money early one morning from one of my carriers who lived in the old Jewish neighborhood, now entirely black. I'd rung his doorbell but had to wait for him to unlock the door. As I waited I noticed what looked like a cocoon lodged in the doorpost, and realized it was a many-times-painted-over mezuzah. I brushed it with my fingers and for the briefest fragment of a moment, as if phone wires had briefly crossed, I could sense all the community who had lived there. I know this sounds goofy but it was a profoundly moving experience, although not a scary one. I've heard terms like genetic memory. I didn't know what to do about it. I started reading. The more I read, the more I wanted to read. How on earth could my father have given this up?

I converted three years ago, just before my birthday. I still sometimes feel inept but a lot more comfortable as a Jew than I did as an Episcopalian. It's like one big piece of a puzzle that has hooked together a lot of other pieces.

Sincerely, Pauline Averbach

Scientific research into genes, personality, and memory is being conducted in several professional venues, but there is no scientific evidence that specific memories are inherited. Thus, there is no reason to suppose that a person can be born "remembering" that he is of Jewish descent, even though so many people told me they instinctively knew they were Jewish. As behavior geneticist Tim Tully of the Cold Spring Harbor Laboratory so succinctly put it, "an instinct does not a memory make."

Dean Hamer, Chief of Gene Structure and Regulation at the National Institutes of Health Laboratory of Biochemistry in Washington, D.C., stresses the significant role genetics plays in identity formation. "Since the discovery of the 'gay gene,' my lab has gone on to find genes for two other personality traits: novelty [thrill] seeking and worry." He chuckled when asked about the possible existence of a Jewish gene. I told him about the people who said they always sensed they were Jewish before they found out for certain.

Interesting question! I agree with Tim Tully that the idea of a "memory gene" is unlikely; I can't imagine what the mechanism would be. On the other hand, I am not at all surprised that many people of Jewish ancestry have a sense that this is the case even when it is unknown to them. In fact, this is just what happened to me. I did not find out until I was twenty-two years old that my paternal grandmother was Jewish. Her father was a rabbi, but unfortunately her husband was anti-Semitic. Yet, as a kid, I always preferred Jewish friends, and even today many people assume I am Jewish.

One possible explanation is that there are certain "Jewish characteristics" (I have no idea what they might be!) that have a genetic basis, and that these are recognized even when one's ancestry has been hidden.

Experimental psychologist Bill Whitlow of Rutgers University expanded on that intriguing remark when I asked him to help me understand why instinct would not be an example of genetic memory. He gave me some models of instinct from the animal world, and then connected that area to this subject.

Sea turtles learn the smell of their birthing place on the beach, and when they're ready to lay their eggs, they swim preferentially back to the smell of the riverbed from which they came. The question we should be asking is not, how did they know to go back to that place, because we already know that place was imprinted on their memory as newborns. The question is, what reactivates that memory in the animal? This activity suggests an important chemical reaction that reactivates memory.

You can look to the social insect world for more examples of instinct. Ants, for instance, perform complex tasks without any acquired instruction. They seem to respond on the basis of inborn behavior patterns. But I strongly doubt those patterns are a memory in the sense that we speak of memories.

People may gravitate toward other people who have either certain physical characteristics or chemical characteristics or behavior characteristics. It's not that they remember them, but there may be a tendency to associate with other individuals who have a shared genetic history. There is, for instance, kinship among mice, which is determined partly by smell, and smell is carried by genes. The past five or six years have seen a fair amount of work trying to unravel this puzzle. There seems to be a genetic basis for certain odor preferences. I wouldn't call it a memory, but it has an impact on which mice feel comfortable with which other mice. There is a lot of discussion as to whether people are similarly influenced, but I don't think there is yet any compelling evidence.

Whitlow's theory called to mind Zigy Kaluzny, who phoned me eight months after our original interview to tell me he was just back from Europe, where he had been astounded by his ability to identify who was Jewish and who was not. He did not go so far as to say it was a mystical gift, but definitely an "almost physical intensity that for me produces closeness and familiarity. I *recognize* the other."

Not everyone I spoke to reported a feeling of recognition when they found out they were of Jewish descent. Many were not particularly shocked or moved or thrilled or distressed. The uncovering of Jewish roots was no more meaningful to them than if they had found out they were part Aleutian or of Buddhist descent. "Depending who I'm with, I identify myself that way. With WASPs I'm WASPy, with Jews I'm

Jewish." "I don't think it changed my views of myself; rather it opened up the roots of where my 'self' had come from." If Jewishness is not an especially charged quality, whether negatively or positively, for the person who uncovers his Jewish ancestry, there is no call for a dramatic response.

Peter Roberts was sixty when he was contacted by his ninety-three-year-old uncle from Jerusalem. Raised as a Unitarian, he responded to the intellectual content of Judaism, and has been drawn to learn more and more about it.

Judaism made no claims to understanding cosmology. The fact is, God is essentially unknowable. But there are ethical and religious premises. Look at the difference in a life based on those premises and one that is not. The Jewish perspective is of a partnership with God. If you think He's justice, then do justice. There have been entire nations that were sick with the absence of God, and look what happened.

I saw through my reading that, in spite of the sexist rap Judaism gets today, if you look at the early texts, there is not only protection for women when other cultures didn't, but humane treatment of animals, of slaves. They were so inclusive—you don't have to be Jewish to be righteous. In the Ten Commandments, you see the underpinning for an absolute morality, and people who seriously try to carry that through and be decent. Originally I, like others, saw ritual observances as strange. But when you view them in the context of a surrounded nation and maintaining identity (a whole other issue), you see things very differently. I found it all very powerful. I joke with my Unitarian friends that Judaism is like Unitarianism on steroids.

Briton Roderick Young never saw a Jew, so far as he knew, until his student days at Oxford University. When his octogenarian aunt Thea disclosed that the family was Jewish and not Episcopalian, Young ran to the nearest synagogue and rang the doorbell, yelling, "I think I'm a Jew and I don't know what to do about it!" Today, years after Roderick successfully researched his genealogy and embarked on a course of study that led to rabbinic ordination, he serves as an assistant rabbi in New York City.

What accounts for the vast range in reactions from the blasé to the dumbstruck? Anselm Strauss explains, "A change must be deemed important before it and kindred changes can be perceived as *vitally* important."[6]

Psychologist Elke Epstein suggests that the more comfortable a person is with her identity, the less pressing her need to grasp at potential change. People who are at relative peace with themselves may simply absorb a new fragment of information and move on, making no significant alterations in self-image. Conversely, a person in search of a clearer sense of who she is will be more motivated to explore new avenues of identity, new possibilities. Adoptees, who often struggle with the "who am I" question, may be more prone to wrestle with new information, but, like anyone else, if they have resolved their questions about identity, or never raised those questions, they will have minimal reaction to finding out they are of Jewish ancestry.

So, which is it? Which makes a person Jewish: memories or genes? Blintzes or biochemicals? Consent or descent? Arguments can be made for either, neither, all or some. The Jewish establishment has criteria that invoke both consent and descent. As mentioned earlier, Orthodox and Conservative Judaism define as Jewish either a sincere convert or the child of a Jewish mother. Reform Judaism recognizes both converts and the child of either Jewish parent, so long as the child expresses interest in identifying with the Jewish people. The criteria are critical at covenantal events: circumcisions, weddings, burials.

Judging by my readings, by the stories I heard, and by my own personal experience, people think of Jewish identity as some or all of the factors that have been mentioned: theology, lineage, culture, Israel, Holocaust, community, education. When I think seriously about how I would feel if I were to find out I am not Jewish, I envision being devastated. For me, Judaism is very insular. My children go to a Jewish school, as did my husband, my siblings, and I. I know that on Friday night I will set the table with a white cloth and my best dishes, and my family will talk over dinner about the week's events and about what we studied. On any other night of the week, we will eat separately, at different times, maybe in different locations. I know that in the spring my parents will visit and we will hold a Seder together. In the fall, I will fast for twenty-five hours, and think hard about how I behaved the past year, and how I plan to change my ways next year. This regimentation gives me some small sense of control in a seemingly haphazard universe. It gives me scripts to follow when words fail. To find out this was not my genuine legacy would be an unspeakable trauma. Surely the same would hold true for a devout Christian or Moslem.

I had started out with a driving curiosity about what it is like suddenly to find out you are of Jewish descent. What I take for granted, these people were encountering for the first time. What I have been studying formally and informally all my life, these people were only just hearing about. What for me is a coat I never take off, these people were seeing as a patchwork of threads. They all began with the discovery of descent, followed by elements of consent. Some came to Judaism because of relatives who died in the Holocaust, some because of a moving visit to Israel, some out of rebellion against parental falsehoods. As someone who was born into a very Jewish household, I was eager to know what it is like to turn a corner and—boom!—come face to face with a wall of Jewishness. The wall is high, and many people were overwhelmed. Some turned away, some scaled the wall, and some looked for a way around it.

What I heard were different definitions of what it means to be Jewish and different reactions to the news, some more dramatic than others. The people I spoke with were serious, introspective thinkers who worked hard at synthesizing their family history with their personal identity because they wanted very much to arrive at closure, identity being such a basic need and entitlement.

As Peter Nash wrote in an essay about his recaptured family history: "What this discovery has done for me is to affirm my already deep conviction that this nation's racial and ethical problems are not, by and large, the product of too much particularism, too much reliance on distinct cultural identities, but rather the tragic consequence of trivializing, discouraging and generally underestimating the fundamental human need for such particularisms."[7]

That was essentially what I saw when I surveyed the expanse of these interviews. When viewed as a whole, staring the way you do at a computer-generated stereogram which gradually develops depth and reveals an underlying picture, what emerges is that their common texture derived from the need for identity.

Perhaps the most encompassing and positive conclusion regarding the phenomenon of recovered heritage came from Paul Goldreich, whose last remark to me was, "Nine times out of ten, finding out who you are is the most life-affirming adjustment you can make."

NOTES

INTRODUCTON

1. Kati Marton, "Making Peace with the Past," in *Newsweek*, 17 February 1997, 44.

2. Erik Erikson, *Dimensions of a New Identity* (New York: W.W. Norton & Co., 1974), 27.

3. Michael A. Meyer (*Jewish Identity in the Modern World* (Seattle: University of Washington Press, 1990), 6.

4. Otto Maduro, email to the author May 22, 1998. Indeed, Maduro, raised as a Catholic, recently learned that his surname is a common one among Jews who fled the Spanish Inquisition.

5. Jonathan Sarna, conversation with the author, June 3, 1998.

6. Report of the Committee on Patrilineal Descent on the Status of Children of Mixed Marriages, resolution adopted by the Central Conference of American Rabbis at its 1983 convention, March 15, 1983.

7. Babylonian Talmud Tractate Kiddushin, 68B, line 7.

8. Anselm A. Strauss, *Mirrors and Masks: The Search for Identity* (New Brunswick: Transaction Publishers, 1997), 152.

CRYPTO-JEWS (PAGES 20–36)

1. Hindquarters are very difficult to render kosher.

2. That was either a gesture of respect to the mezuzah, the verses of Scripture encased in a holder nailed to the doorpost, or an attempt not to be caught cleaning in preparation for the Sabbath.

3. Seth Kunin, "Problems and Possibilities in Crypto-Judaic Studies," *Ha-Lapid* 5, no. 3 (Summer 1998): 2.

4. Gitlitz's *Secrecy and Deceit: The Religion of the Crypto-Jews* (Philadelphia: Jewish Publication Society, 1996) is a premier source on crypto-Jewish history, customs, and beliefs.

5. Messianic Judaism is a form of Christianity, which, like the Jews for Jesus movement, believes in Jewish tradition with the addition of Jesus as the Messiah.

6. Many crypto-Jewish families traditionally had their oldest son enter the priesthood as another sign of loyalty to the Church.

7. Joachim Prinz, *The Secret Jews* (New York: Random House, 1977), 128.

HIDDEN CHILDREN (PAGES 45–71)

1. Eva Fogelman, "Religious Transformation and Continuity," *The Hidden Child: Newsletter of the Hidden Child Foundation/ADL* 7, no. 1 (Fall/Winter 1997): 3.

2. Simone Weil, quoted in Helen Epstein, *Where She Came From: A Daughter's Search for Her Mother's Identity* (Boston: Little, Brown & Company, 1997).

3. Fogelman, 3.

4. At the end of the interview, I asked Stefa what happened to them. The man died young, soon after Stefa's departure; the grandmother, too; and the mother, left alone, killed herself.

5. Fogelman, 3.

CHILDREN OF SURVIVORS (PAGES 72–84)

1. Helen Epstein, *Children of the Holocaust: Conversations with Sons and Daughters of Survivors* (New York: G. P. Putnam's Sons, 1979).

2. Joseph Campbell is the author of the *Historical Atlas of World Mythology*. Rosicrucianism is a belief system based on esoteric wisdom and the secrets of nature, begun by a society of philosophers in the late seventeenth and early eighteenth centuries.

ADOPTEES (PAGES 99–105)

1. Thomas Bouchard, Jr., D. T. Lykken, M. McGue, N. S. Segal, A. Tellegan, "Sources of Human Psychological Difference: The Minnesota Study of Twins Reared Apart," *Science*, no. 250 (1990).

2. David Brodzinsky, Marshall D. Schechter and Robin Marantz Henig, *Being Adopted: The Lifelong Search for Self* (New York: Doubleday, 1992), 12 and 151.

CONCLUSIONS (PAGES 116–126)

1. Gabrielle Glaser, *Strangers to the Tribe: Portraits of Interfaith Marriage* (Boston: Houghton Mifflin Company, 1997).

2. Robert Krell, "Facing Memories: Silent No More," in *The Hidden Child: Newsletter of the Hidden Child Foundation/ADL* 5, no. 1 (Spring 1995): 6.

3. Leon Festinger, *A Theory of Cognitive Dissonance* (Stanford: Stanford University Press, 1957).

4. Anselm A. Strauss, 149.

5. Carl Jung and Herbert Read, *Collected Works of C. G. Jung*, vol. 9 (Princeton: Princeton University Press, 1968).

6. Strauss, 147.

7. Peter Nash, email to the author, November 21, 1997.

Library of Congress Cataloging-in-Publication Data

Kessel, Barbara, 1950–
Suddenly Jewish: Jews raised as Gentiles discover their Jewish roots / Barbara Kessel.
p. cm.— (Brandeis series in American Jewish history, culture, and life)
Includes bibliographical references.
ISBN 1-58465-038-9 (cloth : alk. paper)
1. Jews—Identity. 2. Children of ex-Jews—Interviews. 3. Marranos—Interviews. 4. Jewish children in the Holocaust—Interviews. 5. Children of Holocaust survivors—Interviews. 6. Adopted children—Interviews. 7. Adoption—Religious aspects—Judaism. 8. Judaism—20th century. I. Title. II. Series.

DS 143 .K46 2000
305.892'4073—dc21 99-88877